In the Desert ... With God

Paul Bizeau

Pearl Acres Press

ISBN-13: 979-8-9875146-1-0

Also available as an ebook.

CONTENTS

ACKNOWLEDGMENTS

I am grateful for the help I received in editing this book. My daughter Amanda Nicol used her writing talents to give the early draft of the manuscript a thorough review. JoEllen Claypool (Valley Walker Press) provided the final manuscript edit. Their comments and corrections were important in getting the details right for publication.

Also, to the Idaho Creative Authors Network (ICAN), thanks for your continued encouragement over the last several years as I stumbled toward completion of this project. It has been a blessing to be associated with this group of authors who joyfully share their hard-earned lessons in the self-publishing world with novices like me.

Finally, the writing of this book has been a long journey that could not have been completed without the encouragement of my wife, Glenna. Thank you for the times you were a sounding board when I needed to talk about some of the book's content and the arduous process of publishing.

PREFACE

"He turns a wilderness into pools of water, and dry land into springs. There He makes the hungry dwell, that they may establish a city for a dwelling place and sow fields and plant vineyards, that they may yield a fruitful harvest," (Psalm 107: 35 -37).

I have lived in deserts most of my life. The high desert of Wyoming was home to my family for nearly a quarter century not far from the banks of the Green River. Wander no more than a half mile in any direction from that stream and you were in nothing but sagebrush as far as the eye could see. Yet a few people found a way to live and some to prosper in that land. As a child and later in life, I lived in and around Boise, Idaho which to the casual observer would not seem to qualify as desert with cropland everywhere you drive. Even where I lived in central Washington for a few years, there is abundant agriculture. But it's all artificial . . . irrigated by man's God-given ability to tame nature. A look at the history of these areas reveals that both were barren lands only a century ago and now provide food for the whole world. But they are still deserts. Also, I have been privileged to spend much time in some of the most remote wilderness areas of the western United States, mostly with family, but sometimes all alone. Though these were recreational pursuits, I also learned valuable lessons that relate to a desert journey in life's rough patches.

Knowing something about life in the desert has worked itself into a metaphor for me. This book is born of disappointment and trials, but it is only part of a life that has also experienced blessing. I use many life experiences here to show how God deals with us personally. Like all who know Yahweh through His revealed Word (and the Word became flesh, who dwelt among us), *understanding*

iii

His will and purpose is sometimes not as easy as believing that He is near and has a direction for our lives. The important thing to keep in mind always is that along the way and in the end, all must be for His glory and to honor Him or it is for naught. Solomon's writing in Ecclesiastes shows how the vanities of life should drive us to a closer walk with our creator. My little book is intended to show how the deserts of life can be the time for more intimacy with God.

I am sure that many people have experienced the same or very similar things—things that perplex us or perhaps cause us to question our faith in God. Since mine is a story of the desert, my focus is on the times when life becomes desolate. Meaning and purpose in the pursuits of life, even in the kingdom of God, seem to dry up in ways we have no control over no matter how hard we work or try to avoid them. They come upon us in seasons of life like a hot, dry wind that parches the landscape.

It seems few in our day want to take the time or effort to understand a person's story in life. Story is valuable, though. Even when you are occupied with the pressures of your job, your finances, your family . . . it is important to figure out how God is dealing through the events of your life.

Part of our story is the many struggles that we face; even the decisions that sometimes lead us to bad outcomes. But God desires to etch something even from those events. The hopeful thread in this book is the lesson that the path to a deeper relationship with our God leads often through the deserts of life. I guess that spills the beans. That is, that I believe in a God who created us for personal relationship with Him and not to have just religious experiences. And He brought me to the point of understanding that whether this writing gets outside the four walls of my house is up to Him. What it accomplishes between me and Him is the most important thing.

Mine has been a journey at times into the deep valley of despair and doubting which will help illustrate this journey we call 'life's desert.' It is meant to encourage the believer, but it might also challenge the skeptic. Whether believer or skeptic, we are all prone to ask the question, "Why?" when things don't go as we planned or when, on a larger scale, atrocities or tragedies occur all over the planet. We do this because we are made in the image of God; thus, we have an ingrained desire for justice.

I am not a writer by talent, trade, or profession. I started this writing project in the winter of 2012 with a nudge from the Holy Spirit (He does that in our lives). I had just begun a new chapter in life that seemed to be filling up with desert themes. Little by little, it progressed into what is before you now. Since by its very nature, a desert trek is solitary, so is writing and the two go hand in hand. I earned my living in the engineering profession, working in these desert places where God has molded and shaped me through experiences that I still don't completely understand. But in it all, as long as we let Him speak through His Word, He writes on the pages of our lives (we are His workmanship; Gr. *poiema*, i.e., the artwork of God as stated in Paul's letter to the Ephesians). By that I mean daily to eat the bread of life; that is, "every word that proceeds from God" even when we don't feel like it, even when life's busyness tries to pull us away, even when life's defeats and difficulties discourage our faith. When we put our lives together with scripture and meditate on it, God reveals truths that we would otherwise miss.

In this treatise, do I presume that we find answers to all the harsh realities of life? No. With experience, we learn that unfortunate things happen sometimes because of our own poor choices, sometimes because of others' choices that we had no control over, and sometimes in the grace and purpose of God alone. In those times, if we are attentive and, like Jacob, are willing to wrestle with God, we get real, practical theology. It is my intent to relate, not great hidden truths, but what I believe God would have me share of one man's journey of faith. In the desert times of life, you see more clearly that the world is a broken place while experiencing the brokenness of your own life.

This is a book whose audience would more likely be people of faith in Christ because it is steeped in biblical references. It also includes things I picked up from other writers that have helped build my worldview and my faith. But those who don't share that same faith go through deserts too. To them I say, read and see what God wants to do. This book will not change your life. Only God can do that. And chiefly, He is in the business of reconciling mankind to Himself (2 Corinthians 5:19). I pray you will be open to this and will accept His offer. King David said it well: "Oh, taste and see that the Lord is good. Blessed is the man who trusts in Him," (Psalm 34:8).

CHAPTER 1

ENTERING LIFE'S DESERTS

It began after being laid off in the spring of 2010 (along with many good folks) from a 'dream job' I held for over four years as a staff engineer with the state parks agency in Idaho, a consequence of the economic crisis that began a year earlier. It came to me all at once lying in bed one night and then recurring many times thereafter. On that first night, the enemy gripped me with all the criticisms I could recall from years past. At night, we are most vulnerable to the devil's accusations. As my wife was falling asleep, he brought them to mind, one by one. It wouldn't have worked any other way. A man can survive, even forgive himself for one or two mistakes in his life . . . if he can forget the rest of them. But failure at the thing that defines men most—their work—causes a vicious cycle of fear leading to self-doubt that comes back again and again. All the enemy needs to do is inject a thought or bring up some unresolved conflict and a battle for the mind and spirit of a man is underway. Fear of failure is an unhealthy way to live, but very real. I try to remind myself of the way Thomas Edison looked at failure—as a means of finding out what *didn't* work, but it is different when a man sees himself as a failure in the eyes of others . . . whether real or perceived. It is a kind of shame that makes you want to hide under a rock. It was the beginning of a desert season in life.

As you read this, you might be going through a desert. It might be a Sahara—a long, wide expanse, where the heat is intense every day. You get the feeling that it will never end as you are forced to traverse its expanse. Or it may be like the Red Desert of Wyoming––small by comparison to most others but with long, cold winters that are equally hard to survive. You may be going through these wilderness years while still a young adult. Some don't experience them until the last years of their lives when loneliness and isolation settle in like a cloud. One thing I have learned is that God speaks through the experience if we have ears to hear. To be sure, I am not talking about the midlife crisis where a man suddenly realizes that he has not lived life to the fullest so he goes on a fling or spends his life savings on a Porsche. I also am not referring to those personal crisis moments in life that bring great emotional, physical, or financial pain.

A Desert Just For You

The people of early Israel referred to deserts by degrees. First, there was _midbar_ - not green and lush, but with enough vegetation for animals to survive. Next there is _arabah_ - so named after the region between the Dead Sea and the Gulf of Aqaba. You can dig a well for water and survive with some help. Lastly, there is _jeshimon_ wherein the only way to survive is by God's provision. Otherwise, you stay out. The Arabian Desert is like this (and even Antarctica). Abraham's route to the Promised Land required a long detour around this area. The remote parts of Sinai are like this. Hence, when the children of Israel were there, God had to provide manna for them to survive. It is inhospitable. Without question, life in the desert is roughing it. You are camping. No one builds a house there.

So jeshimon is the place you don't want to be, but it's the only place where you are entirely dependent on God . . . where God has you to Himself, so to speak. I have found myself at times complaining to God that He has brought an end to friendships built through the years and put great distance between me and family in this desert experience; even in the church, struggling to approach people and establish what should be the most normal and healthy of relationships as part of the body of Christ. When people are gone, we get fearful because we think we are lost and abandoned. Yet He keeps reminding us of purpose . . . that nobody lives in jeshimon; only God is there for you. It seems like a borderless expanse in the absence of familiar faces, but God intends it to be a place where your trust in Him becomes unequivocal.

Let's face it. Sometimes we find ourselves in the wilderness by the shove of human hands, perhaps in a fit of their own exasperation. It might present itself in other people's envy or evil intent toward us. Or it might just be passive aggressiveness in their actions that eventually changes the environment in which you live from green pasture to desert. Remember the story of Hagar in Genesis chapter 16. The Bible shows the desperate measures taken by Sarah to have a family by insisting that Abraham have sexual relations with one who was not his wife, but the servant of Sarah—probably much younger and certainly of childbearing age (unlike Sarah who was 77 years old then). Can anyone reasonably imagine that this was the will of God? Of course not! We all know that Abraham should have put the kibosh on that idea immediately. It shows how weak men can be at times when God wants faith and leadership from us.

When Hagar conceived, it just made Sarah angrier at God. Of all people, she took it out on her husband, who then further abdicated by not defending the poor woman. We are told that Sarah deals harshly with Hagar who then runs away. Obviously in this part of the world, it's not a long journey into inhospitable wilderness, especially foreboding for a pregnant woman. No doubt she would have perished on her own. But who shows up? None other than Jesus, revealed here as the Angel of the Lord. He sees the injustice done to her. He tells her to go back to Sarah. I believe it is here that she comes to trust the Lord personally. It is beautifully written in verse 13 where she says, "You are the God who sees me." Without

3

knowing the mercy of the Lord, she would not have been able to submit to Sarah again. Only thirteen years later she would be forced to leave for good and, once again, be found in the desert, without hope, giving up on life and believing that her end was near. But Jesus shows up again to save her. God wants to show Himself personally to us in the deserts of our lives. Do you know God as the one who sees you day after day?

With that in mind, consider the necessity of a wilderness experience in our lives as God's calling in order to become whole in Christ. Though we think of Paul starting out a firebrand for the Gospel, he really wasn't a ready vessel in God's eyes, so we read (only briefly, but importantly in Galatians 1:17) that he went to Arabia. We are not told how long he was there. We can only conjecture, but we have the important clue that he "did not immediately confer with flesh and blood . . ." and that he did not go to the disciples in Jerusalem. What does that tell you? I think, as some do, that he spent many days alone with Jesus in prayer. It is also possible that this is the very time and place where much of the theology revealed in the New Testament was developed, only later to be written in Paul's letters to the churches. He escaped the Jews in Damascus whose intention it was to kill him. The wonder is that he came back to that same place for three years. No doubt in the duration of his desert experience, God not only had Paul for some important time of communion, but He was at work to remove the threat on Paul's life in Damascus. He is also at work in our situations to arrange things we are not quite ready for at the time.

What about the life of Moses? We learn from the Scripture that his formative years were lived in Pharaoh's court with all the privilege, power and protection that came with it. You would think his heart of compassion for his own people would be rewarded by God and countrymen. Instead, his zeal for justice leads to a murder rap, and he was forced into a desert exile that would last an unbelievable forty years! That is a big chunk of time out of life that seems mostly unproductive on the surface. I don't think God condoned the murder of an Egyptian taskmaster, but He is always working things for good and to fulfill His purposes (Romans 8:28). Instead of leading a nation out of Egypt in his youth, God sent him to the most mundane of existences hundreds of miles away on the back side of a Midian desert near the Gulf of Aqaba (modern Saudi Arabia). Here, he took a wife, started a family and tended to his father-in-law's sheep business. In the naming of his first son, Gershom, we get a strong hint about how all of this made him feel– –like a stranger in a foreign country.

By this time, Moses' religious background was quite diverse being raised in the Egyptian system of Sun worship though strongly influenced by his Hebrew mother and now living with the Priest of Midian and whatever religion that entailed. Just as with Paul, we are not told how God dealt with Moses in those forty years. We don't know about his spiritual journey until God reveals Himself in the burning bush. Before this, I don't think Moses had any thought of returning to Egypt and he certainly tried to argue God out of the idea. When I ponder the story of Moses, I am always drawn to what it must have been like to give up the good life just to survive in the desert.

As it relates to my life, I think about how Moses was no longer a young man. Now he is perhaps middle aged in terms of his life span which was unusually long. At the peak of his influence and social position in life, things change overnight. When it goes that way for a man or woman after all he or she has built in status and wealth and any other measure of success, the desert they find themselves in is very unsettling. But here, God is doing a work. The American evangelist Dwight L. Moody once said, "Moses spent the first 40 years of his life becoming something, the next 40 years as a nothing, and the last 40 years learning what God can do with nothing."

Think about Jonah and his sojourn. God told him to go across the northern reaches of the Arabian Desert to Nineveh, perhaps on the King's Highway—an overland trek of about 500 miles. It is outside modern Mosul, Iraq. (If you look at satellite images, you can see incredible archeological digs there.) For its time, Nineveh was a large city, and the travel time for Jonah was easily a month, considering he would not have traveled on Sabbaths. That would have given him plenty of time to hone his message, pray, and boost his courage.

All of this makes me wonder who Jonah was in his day. The narrative gives us a few clues, but we have to conjecture about some things. We aren't told what he did for a living other than prophesy to the people of Israel during the reign of King Jeroboam II. Perhaps his was an ordinary existence out of which God plucked him. Perhaps he was well-known in Israel. We aren't told. God intended one desert journey for the blessing of a nation Jonah did not care for and, in fact, may have feared because of their reputation for ruthlessness. (Their descendants have that reputation even today!) But Jonah chose a different way that ended up in the depths of the wide, open Mediterranean Sea. And his only way back to land was through the belly of a whale and getting belched up on a beach. And he still had a wide expanse of desert to cross from that point!

One theme I take from this account is that even if we try to escape the will of God or a desert journey, God might force it on us. And that can be a frightening prospect. We all know that it would have gone easier for Jonah if he had just followed the original plan. Though no desert journey is intended to be comfortable, you can be sure God has a purpose revealed on the way to the other side. Jonah was probably afraid of many things . . . the language barrier, they wouldn't listen, they certainly wouldn't repent; they might even kill him. Little did he know that God had prepared the hearts of an enemy state for a spiritual awakening, the likes of which perhaps Jonah never saw in all his days of preaching back home.

I suspect that in most situations, people don't think about whether their life is in a desert time. Most would say life happens and we just live it. Does it even matter that we know? I think it is important because purpose is necessary in the human experience. It is depressing to our spirit when we see nothing but emptiness in front of us because we aren't aware of its purpose. The desert might encroach on you gradually or it might swallow you up overnight. We know it by our personal circumstances. Sometimes you come to realize it with the passage of time. It might have nothing to do with your financial situation; you may be financially secure but find that you are staring out at a bleak horizon because you found no meaning from it.

Or there is that feeling of irrelevance one gets from encounters with people. On one such occasion, I was invited to be a Facebook "friend" while discovering that this person could not hold a public conversation with me longer than two minutes before his attention was diverted by his 12 year-old child. Right or wrong, I had the feeling that in the desert, people always have someone more important to be with than you.

It may be just the path you take in life that leads you naturally, at times, through the desert. It might show up as the loss of human relationships for a long season where friends and family seem to forget you exist or have lost compassion for you. In fact, my desert experience seems to come from the ordinary as others would view it. To me, it seemed extraordinary at times. Yours may feel the same.

The verse of hope from Psalm 107 in the preface to this book is followed immediately by a harsh prediction:

> *When they are diminished and brought low through oppression, affliction and sorrow, He pours contempt on princes and causes them to wander in the wilderness where there is no way.* (Psalm 107:39-40)

These verses capture the feeling of one who was riding the wave of good fortune and suddenly is plunged into desolation. The meaning of the word *princes* escapes our western understanding because those titles don't exist much today except as figureheads. The

Hebrew meaning is one who is usually magnanimous or one of generous nobility. He or she is doing well and is doing good for others perhaps, but circumstances change and reversals of fortune reveal that they are not in control . . . and never were. The desert appears at first a very unwelcome place. It isn't where you are used to living because in it one must struggle just to survive. The psalm is about how God alone controls nature and our destiny, and He causes us to cry out to Him as the only one who satisfies our needs.

I wouldn't presume to write this book unless I found myself in the desert journey at times believing that God must have abandoned me, my usefulness to Him somehow gone. Certainly, I say to myself, God does not dwell in the desert. He is with His people in the hustle and bustle of life, right? But no, He shows up in the most desperate times when we are struggling just to survive either emotionally, physically, or spiritually. One thing the deserts of life allow you to do is stop and ponder why you are pursuing what the rest of the world chases after, knowing it could be gone overnight in the next stock-market panic or job loss or any number of events. You catch yourself playing this game though you know you are not in it to win it. We are in the world, but not of the world (that is, the world system). At times, you find yourself fighting to keep from not caring. It is as if you have been starved for so long, nothing matters but your own needs. Yet you know that isn't the way God wants you to live.

In the desert time of life, you experience the feeling that you are largely irrelevant. The culture sweeps past you like a torrential storm, the kind that we are warned about when crossing the dry arroyos of the desert. There, the intense rains are gathered into flood waters, and you suddenly realize you no longer have any influence on it. After all, you are in an isolated place, seemingly alone. You want to have some impact, but you are just a wanderer in a place that is not well mapped. You could jump into the flood at your peril or let God lead you out in His time. But it's tempting to think, "I should be in the current of life, with my influence spreading," all the while you are experiencing a time of diminishment. It's important to remember that this life isn't meant to be defined just by our successes or all the good that happens to us, but also by the failures and deserts we go through. In fact, it may be on this path that God chisels you into someone more useful for His kingdom, a time when you finally lose things you once counted on. Are you inclined to view the desert as a negative experience, especially when you see how it affects your human relationships?

For Moses in exile, for Paul after his Damascus conversion, for David before he was king, can't we conclude that the desert experience, though a trial by fire in some cases, was intended to discipline, correct, or teach? Most people think of it today as a place of banishment, but that really misses its true importance to our lives. American pastor and author A.W. Tozer famously said, "It is certain that God cannot greatly bless a man until He has hurt him deeply."

John Bunyan wrote:

> "Conversion is not the smooth, easy-going process some men seem to think. It is wounding work, of course, this breaking of the hearts, but without wounding, there is no saving. Where there is grafting there is a cutting, the scion must be let in with a wound; to stick it onto the outside or tie it on . . . would be of no use. Heart must be set to heart and back to back or there will be no sap from root to branch and this I say must be done by a wound." (*The Acceptable Sacrifice: The Excellency of a Broken Heart* in the Works of John Bunyan, Vol. 1, public domain)

It is certain that the more years we live, the more hardship and pain and hurt we will experience. Not to say there are not rich blessings mixed in. We should always see those just as clearly. The comparison to the real desert is apparent. Hardly anything grows there. Southern Wyoming is full of bitterbrush, rabbit brush, and sagebrush. But there are also exquisite blooms in the desert. I remember the flower of the prickly pear cactus there, made more beautiful because it is so rare (it doesn't bloom every year). Few animals can survive on the desert diet there. How the antelope do it, I don't understand. And water . . . well, let's just say you better go prepared—carry it with you or you will go for long stretches without it. So when we need a drink, God gives us the "washing of water by the word," (Ephesians. 5:26). It not only cleanses us but satisfies our thirsty souls.

Physical pain is designed by our creator to tell us there is a problem that needs immediate attention . . . or else! In the same way, pain of the soul or heart grabs us, sometimes shaking us to our very foundations. And when it does, what is one of the first things we are reminded to do? "Count it all joy . . ." (James 1:2). Amid our pain or loss, that act seems incomprehensible and the last thing on our mind. But the truth from that scripture can only be applied in times like these. Later, I will get into what I have learned that the scriptures say about trials . . . things I didn't understand at a deeper level until God put me into the pit of suffering; things, of course, I still don't fully understand.

Mature Christians in America might not think much of the 'health and wealth' gospel, but we still get caught up in the mentality that success is highly valued while the dry times of life are not. All over the world, men are conditioned to define themselves by their work and women by marriage and children (also, now the added pressure of physical appeal). Even when we get together as family and friends, what is most of our conversation about? "How is the job going?" or the new car or bragging about the grandkids or a myriad of things that we have been conditioned to obsess over. We should care about what is going on in others' lives, but not forget the biblical admonition to "rejoice with those who rejoice and weep with those who weep" because both happen with regularity in life. Our nature is to avoid doing the latter, I think in large part because we don't value the lessons of the dry times of life. And now in this golden age of internet access, Facebook and Twitter have become the avenues through which we open our lives to others. That most often comes across as artificial, i.e., you see the good side of my life, but not the ugly realities that inevitably occur. Of course, we don't want people to see our failures. That would take away the shiny veneer.

So where did all this come to fruition in my life? And how did these lessons manifest themselves? Like most people, I have worried about how others perceive me in the arena of life, whether through work or wealth. I haven't been very public about it, but it always comes up because our world system has engrained materialism in us. I am unconvinced that different cultures have succeeded in rooting that out (whether through Buddhism or Communism or Socialism or any other 'ism' out there) because it is man's nature to have, to possess, to control instead of being satisfied in God. Don't get me wrong. God doesn't say we shouldn't enjoy life and the things of this life, just that they not become idols and rob Him of glory.

Disappointment With God

Are you like me in thinking that you have had more than your fair share of disappointment in life? It is another experience that comes along with the desert life. Though I have come to understand that God doesn't take us all down the same path, don't we all still feel uncomfortable sharing parts of our story? For me, it is because the experiences of my desert years brought me face to face with shame so intense, it was frightening. I define shame as what you feel about who you are. By contrast, guilt is the feeling you get when you have done something wrong. I think some people have the mistaken belief that if you follow the rules, go to church, tithe, and serve God to the best of your understanding . . . that recipe should result in everyone getting the same deal. It is mistaken because it denies God's sovereignty. It also denies the purpose of suffering which I believe He has used to teach me, in part, not to depend on this world system for satisfaction. Otherwise, I stoop to idol worship with which we in this post-modern age have become acquainted. That is, we seem more bound to our culture than our God.

One of the ways God reveals Himself to us is through the leading of the Holy Spirit. By that, I don't mean He leads us to find the perfect parking spot at the mall. Rather, that He gives us discernment in how we use our spiritual gifts for the kingdom of heaven. Knowing that, still I have been disappointed with Him when my efforts were not received well by people. Even in the writing of this book, I have been disappointed with God when things went wrong along the way. When that has happened to you, have you questioned your faith in Him? Has it created distance between you and God?

In the Bible, the men who journeyed the desert seemed to have at least this in common—God eventually came to them, met with them, finally restoring them to the place of service He intended for them all along. But before He did that, can I conjecture that they, too, experienced some disappointment with God?

I don't claim to have suffered as Job. Like most people who read that oldest of stories in the Bible, I am amazed at the response of Job, at least early in his trials. Before the first chapter is over, he lost his business to raiding barbarians and his children to a freakish storm. His initial response was,

> *The LORD gave, and the LORD has taken away;*
> *blessed be the name of the LORD.* (Job 1:21)

Who among us can say that after taking such a hit? We might be able to if we knew the worst was over, but what if it just keeps coming? Yet, we have this from Job, the perfect example of how to respond in the face of loss in our lives—worship. It is certainly not a natural response. It is a disciplined response. To use a baseball idiom, Job was a man who seemed to cover his bases well (Job 1:5). But he knew his blessings were from God and not a result of his own good character or hard work alone. So how do we respond when

God shakes our lives to the core? As I began this writing effort, I was back to what most would call a period of prosperity and normalcy. But when you have been through tough times, you always know that prosperity is a fickle friend.

For riches certainly make themselves wings; they fly away like an eagle toward heaven. (Proverbs 23:5)

The thing that Job learned was that God gets it right . . . all the time. But before he got there, he voiced considerable disappointment with God. You could say at least God gave him some company, even though those four friends were offering little comfort. When you look at Job's story as a whole, you know God designed it as a Romans 8:18 experience (suffering in this life pales in comparison with future glory) though he couldn't see that when in the middle of it all, considering the shock of losing everything in a short span of time. No doubt, it wounded his spirit deeply to experience such shame in his life. You see, shame, self-imposed or otherwise, is a flesh-eating disease leaving raw wounds exposed, such that you are very reluctant to let others into your life. You try to keep human relationships out. Only the strong-hearted soul can see that and take up the courage to venture close and bring some comfort to the wounded. If there is no one like that coming to you, self-inflicted shame can be perpetuated.

How Long, Lord?

David's early adult life helps us put suffering and trials in perspective. Here was a man who was told as a ruddy youth that he would be the next king of Israel. But he wasn't told he would have to wait 22 years for that to happen and in the meantime endure wandering in the desert to escape the death threats of Saul and the treachery of other foreign enemies in giving up his position to Saul. You see in some of the psalms written by David during this time that he was battling disappointment with God. Psalm 56 is set to the music of a song called "The Silent Dove in Distant Lands." What thoughts that conjures! It seems to speak of the loneliness of David's days then. A dove is not usually silent. If it is, something is wrong. You hear it's cooing in the daytime. Where my wife and I lived in Idaho and Washington, it would be like a silent meadowlark. The bird takes delight in singing its warble all day long. The psalms following that one are set to the tune "Do Not Destroy." His words speak of the pressing need to seek God's deliverance in times when evil surrounds us, but also the need to have this relationship with Him, acknowledging (through praise) who He is, <u>especially</u> when the darkness seems to be closing in.

Why didn't God just wait until he was within a couple of years of the end of Saul's reign? Perhaps partly because in His patience, He was giving Saul time to repent, but also because David needed the preparation of the desert to be ruler, both politically and militarily. And that couldn't be done overnight. Once he assumed the throne, his desire to please God had not been diminished by those harsh years. After conquering Jerusalem, he wanted to bring the Ark of the Covenant there. Filled with joy and happiness at the task, he was about to confront another time of disappointment with God. The story is a familiar one as we see Uzzah struck down for touching a tottering ark. It was a reflexive move. We would say well-intentioned, as was David's work of securing the ark in a new and better place. David became angry about this incident (2 Samuel 6:8 and 1 Chronicles 13:9) and "was afraid of God that day . . ." saying, in effect, "I've tried to please God and look what happened!" In David's mind (and I know in our fleshly thinking as well), God was showing Himself unreasonable and this is disappointing to us.

When I was a young man between jobs with two toddlers and a wife to support, we made the momentous decision to leave a life we had established in Wyoming and go where employment prospects looked better in the northwest. It was a tremendous upheaval in our lives that started with moving a pickup load of our possessions in a solo trip to my brother's place in Oregon and pounding the streets of Portland for employment prospects; then, returning for my family and moving with the rest of our stuff to an apartment complex in a suburb of Seattle. It was a devastating blow to my ego to put my wife in a living situation that I considered next to poverty.

After four months of relentless searching there, I finally landed a job another 200 miles away with a consulting firm. It happened through a headhunter that had only weeks before been completely unknown to me. Though I was glad for the work, it wasn't long before I learned that my new employer was a struggling family-owned engineering firm, somewhat dysfunctional, and whose best days were behind them. It was a sweatshop of sorts with a demanding owner who sometimes preferred to manage me by ridicule. I began to see these two years of my life as a sojourn into Egypt because it felt like the place where God was keeping us during a time of famine more than anything else.

Still, I learned important things in that job, especially the value of putting detail into drawings and construction documents. At the end, God wonderfully opened a door for us to return to Wyoming where we enjoyed many years of prosperity though certainly not without our share of struggles and disappointments.

Don't Waste Your Time

The wilderness years can seem so unproductive, but not wasting them means learning all that God intends for you to learn about Him in those times. This is especially true if we see our contribution to God's kingdom diminished. When God puts you in the desert, you naturally ask the question, "Why don't you want to use me anymore?" I learned that wasting the wilderness years has much less to do with lack of productivity and more with not allowing God to fully use that time in the manner that He desires for us no matter how desolate it seems. We can waste them by whining and complaining as the children of Israel did many times, just wanting to go back where things were stable. How soon they had forgotten that stability also meant bondage! We can waste the years simply by not letting God speak and not having "ears to hear;" i.e., not cultivating discernment of what the Holy Spirit is doing, our teacher and comforter in this life. And I think the desert is where you learn some of that because there you have God or you have nothing at all.

In my desert times, the extent of my influence seemed pathetically small and shrinking. But the better question to ask is: did I do everything I could with what God gave me? Did I fully use opportunities to influence others with the Gospel? Consider John the Baptist. Here was a preacher who lived what would be considered a monkish lifestyle, presumably not preaching in the city—mostly in the plains near the Jordan River. Some have speculated that he was known among the community of Qumran where the Dead Sea Scrolls were found in the 20th century. Because his parents were older when he was born, he might have been raised by people there instead of at home. Yet God used him to speak words which brought many to repentance and even to remind the powerful that God will not be mocked by their immoral and corrupt lifestyles. Because of this boldness in preaching the truth, he was abruptly killed in a most heinous manner by a compromising, licentious politician. Do you think John was well liked? Certainly not by the ruling class. From his life, we can at least learn to be 'John the Baptists' for God in our day and speak for Jesus whose politically incorrect claim is to be the Way, the Truth, and the Life.

What does that kind of witness look like? The apostle Paul used the sense of smell to describe it:

> *Now thanks be to God who always leads us in triumph in Christ, and through us diffuses the fragrance of His knowledge in every place. For we are to God the fragrance of Christ among those who are being saved and among those who are perishing. To the one we are the aroma of death leading to*

death, and to the other the aroma of life leading to life. (2 Corinthians 2:14-16)

There was a fragrance of God's presence that Herod detected in John. That is why I don't think Herod wanted to have him put to death. To his wife, John's witness smelled like death. She couldn't stand his morally convicting words. And so it is with us. Even as desert messengers, we are influencing people. Some think the Christian smells like a rotting corpse. They see Jesus as still in the grave. It is a "smell" that drives them away. Others who are open to the Gospel are smelling resurrection and they are drawn to it.

It took a desert journey of my own to magnify the significance of Jesus' resurrection. A closer look at John's eye-witness account of the resurrection grabbed my attention (The Gospel According to John, chapter 20). Keep in mind as you read the Gospel accounts of the resurrection that Jesus had told His disciples many times that he would be killed, yet rise again on the third day. Like us, I am sure, they put this out of their minds because it was unimaginable. Their rabbi, put to death for teaching about this new and coming kingdom? Besides, this kind of miracle is impossible, right? When Jesus was crucified, they were devastated, just as we would have been if we had witnessed it.

Then Resurrection Sunday starts with Mary Magdalene approaching the tomb while it was still dark outside. Matthew's gospel fills in the detail that she was also with *"the other Mary"* so presumably the mother of James the Lesser. Here is where the original language is captivating. She *"saw"* (*blepo* - to look at or notice) that the stone had been rolled away. They run back to Peter and John to tell them that the Lord's body was not there. These two men run to the tomb with John racing ahead of Peter where he, too, *blepo* from outside the tomb, only noticing that the cloth wrappings were lying there – in the original, literally outstretched, as if the clothes were left in the shape of a body never disturbed, though it was gone. Now, it is Peter's turn. Running past John into the tomb, he "saw" (*theoreo*) the linen clothes as well as the face cloth folded separately. In this word, we learn that the wheels are turning in Peter's head. He is thinking, forming a theory based on all the facts, but he isn't quite there. Back to John as he now enters the tomb and *"saw"* (*eido* - to perceive or understand). Yes, he gets past the theory and believes that the resurrection is bedrock truth. Understanding the first thoughts running through the minds of those who witnessed the resurrection of Jesus filled me with a joy I had not experienced in a while.

The thought occurs to me of the battle of the mind that goes on when you are deep in the desert and you feel your significance waning. I am tempted to think this by little things that have occurred, but they keep adding to the weighty sum of indignities endured—a slight by someone you barely know at work; other younger men passing over you for the more prestigious work assignments; or someone you know asking for your professional advice only to find out later they disregarded it after you had put in considerable time and effort. People seem to treat you with less respect, even children. Shortly after I started writing this book, I decided to get involved with helping boys grow in their knowledge of the Bible through a church sponsored memorization and teaching class. I did it because a dearth in the knowledge of God was evident in our young people. I discovered that Satan (henceforth, I will refer to him as the enemy) fights hard to spoil this effort. I found myself largely ineffective and disrespected. I kept at it for two school years because I didn't want to sit on the bench. God wants to use even those days we are just trudging through the wilderness.

The fight is, at its root, a fleshly one in which you must learn that your desire for significance and honor or even some acceptance among people is not important when placed next to the Gospel. The longing and pursuit for significance of any kind can also be a form of idolatry in our modern age. So put down this desire of the flesh to be known and loved by others because our role in the kingdom, however we perceive it, is to bring honor and glory to God. Even as people, quite naturally, do not venture out into the desert to be with us, we need to be thankful for what He is doing through them for the advancement of the kingdom. All that we have relied on in ourselves is to be put down.

> . . . *casting down arguments and every high thing that exalts itself against the knowledge of God, bringing every thought into captivity to the obedience of Christ.* (2 Corinthians 10:5)

'Arguments' in this verse is from the original *logismos* which is literally 'computation' (think logically) and figuratively 'reasoning.' It is our nature to want to figure everything out, but God says we must stop doing that. The Scottish teacher and missionary Oswald Chambers wrote,

> "God will never reveal more truth about Himself until you have obeyed what you know already. Beware of becoming "wise and prudent." (*My Utmost For His Highest, Classic Edition,* Oswald Chambers, copyright 1935, Dodd, Mead & Company, New York, Fifty-fourth printing, from October 10 reading; public domain)

Where Did My Strength Go?

My childhood years read like a story book—so many good experiences and fun adventures, thanks in large part to the sacrifices and love of my parents. I never really knew what hardship was all about. The lessons of suffering didn't take root until my early adult life and didn't really come to fruition until later; in fact, at what seemed to me a most inconvenient time in life when I had established a path to follow, even to the best of my understanding the will of God. It came at a time when a great deal of the strength of my youth had already been expended in achieving my plans. It came when I was in my mid 50s—a time when most people find it difficult to start over.

The realization that your body is aging is both awakening and unwelcome. Let me illustrate with two wilderness experiences that occurred in the same place for me but nearly 25 years apart. After being married just two years, my wife and I joined my dad and several brothers in the summer of 1982 for a backpacking trip into the Eagle Cap Wilderness in northeast Oregon. We were there for most of a week, the destination being a small lake (Pop Lake) eight miles from the trailhead . . . nearly all uphill. Now, you must know my wife to appreciate any of this. She was not the outdoorsy type growing up and had never camped in a tent before marrying me. But I have learned that she is game for almost any adventure where she can experience the beauty and grandeur of God's creation. We lagged everyone else in the party who had arrived at the lake hours before us and were already fishing and setting up camp. We had our own maps and made it to the lake in plenty of time before evening, but the hike includes about two miles of sketchy, unmaintained trail over a ridge. It was challenging, and we were tired when we got there, but we were young and not much worse for the wear. Besides, I got to demonstrate my map-reading prowess and Boy Scout trail skills to my new bride.

Fast forward 24 years when my son, now 23, unexpectedly says he would like to go on a backpack trip with me as part of a visit to our new home in Nampa, Idaho. I say unexpectedly because I thought I had burned out my kids on the idea of camping and hiking years earlier. The Eagle Cap was only a four-hour drive from Nampa, and I had longed for years to see that idyllic place once more. My son was a strapping young man who could easily carry a 50-pound pack. I was in adequate shape physically, having a semi-regular routine of walking the dog and bike riding. I thought it possible that we could make the same hike in one day because my distant memory had convinced me that it was only a short jaunt over the ridge to Pop Lake once you got off the trail. We left the house early on an August morning. I recall being at the trailhead by noon with a long summer day ahead of us. But after hiking only the first five miles and arriving at the trail jump-off point, we were forced to camp by the arrival of evening with insufficient daylight remaining to reach our destination. I was also physically wrung out from the uphill climb.

The next morning, I looked up at the hike before us and wondered why it looked so far to the ridge top. I didn't remember it that way, but thought a two or three-hour hike would get us there in time for a full day of fishing. Instead, it took six hours. I was moving slow when we got there, but the trek was worth it. (I have another life lesson from that short trip, but it is for a later chapter). We thought we might stay for two days and enjoy ourselves, but an unexpected cold front moved in early the next morning with dark, threatening clouds. I feared that we might get snowed in because at that elevation, nasty weather is possible even in late August. It is unlike me to go unprepared for such a situation, but I confess that I didn't have any rain gear and only a sweatshirt to keep me warm at night. We quickly ate breakfast, broke camp, and began our hike out in the rain, reaching the top of the ridge above the lake when my fears were realized.

Wet snow was beginning to soak our clothes with temperatures now in the mid-thirties. A mix of snow and rain continued, and by the time we reached the trail barely two hours later, I was soaked and shivering. My son advised that we continue without stopping as there wasn't any dry wood for a fire and little chance of drying out if the storm were to continue throughout the day. By the time we reached the valley below, I was shivering uncontrollably with over an hour still before we would reach the trailhead and the warmth of my pickup. I was literally on the verge of hypothermia, ashamed that I could have put us both in that much peril. I had never been in a situation like this with all my years of experience in the wilderness. It took us six hours to get out with a lot of downhill now wearing on my knees and adding to my difficulty. This story illustrates how the years wear us down in ways we don't recognize until we get to the edge of the desert and realize only too late that we might not have the strength to get across.

How do we go on when our strength fails us, when our emotional, physical, and even spiritual resources are seemingly near exhaustion? I got to this point several times in the desert journey beginning when I was only 53. Believe it or not, God sometimes calls us to a season in life like this where it seems that everyone and everything seems to abandon us in order that we may come out of the mad busyness that occupies our days to seek Him and know Him. Amazingly, we learn that God is in that most inhospitable of places. Even more, we find how shallow our knowledge of Him was before that. Here, Psalm 84 is helpful to the weary traveler. I grew to love the imagery of this psalm, and we memorized it as a family when our children were still young. Written by the "sons of Korah" (they were the worship leaders of the tribe of Levi in Israel, from which the priests came), it is poetry about the real longing in life's dry spells that can only be satisfied by God. How else can you explain the writers' words?

> *My soul* (spirit) *longs . . . even faints . . . My heart* (emotional center) *and my flesh* (physical being) *cry out for the living God.* (Psalm 84:2, parentheses mine)

It is about the people of God on a trek through the wilderness to the city of God and, eventually, its sanctuary where they would finally experience God's presence.

> *Blessed is the man whose strength is in You, whose heart is set on pilgrimage.* (Psalm 84:5)

The child of God must realize that this life is a pilgrimage on the way to heaven. Your heart must be settled on that fact. If it isn't, you will be double-minded, one day wanting the temporary comforts and things of this earthly existence and the next day, pining for heaven when you don't get them.

If you are in a desert stretch of life, you also need God's strength to get through it.

> *As they pass through the valley of Baca, they make it*
> *a spring; the rain also covers it with pools.* (Psalm
> 84:6)

The Hebrew root for Baca has to do with "weeping," so perhaps this was an actual location where water only seeped from the rocks, a place in the journey with almost no potable water sources. But when you are thirsty, its water gives you hope and refreshment. This could be symbolic of those times we are crying inside. The journey is now through places where it even seems that God is silent. You feel alone, without anyone who cares; yet God sustains you with just what you need. Have you ever been on a trail crossing over solid rock? Oftentimes, you only know it is there from cairns left by previous hikers. It is comforting to know that others have been on that same journey. Over time, little shallow basins have formed where water from even a small rainstorm fills them. Notice they are not creeks or lakes. They are not big bodies of water; just enough to refresh you or your trusty pack animal. Then you are on your way. You can't linger. I like the translation of *"pools"* here because of the imagery it conveys, but the Hebrew is from "barak," meaning 'bless' and is used many times in the Psalms. Either way, it is these little blessings that encourage us when we most need it.

Finally,

> *They go from strength to strength; each one appears*
> *before God in Zion.* (Psalm 84:7)

The original word for strength here is different than that of verse 5. It has more to do with a man's means or an army's force. That is, when God has refreshed us, we can muscle our way through the crags and up the steep hills, eventually arriving at our destination . . the very presence of God. There is nothing wrong with thinking that God expects us to get up and keep going with a mind and will even through the toughest travels. John Phillips states it well in his commentary on this passage:

> "Sometimes we wonder if we will make it; the way is so hard and rough. There are disappointments, dangers, and difficulties. But over and over again, when it seems that we must be overwhelmed, we get our second wind. God supplies new grace and we get strength to go on." (Taken from *Exploring Psalms, Vol. 1,* © copyright 2002 by John Phillips. Published by Kregel Publications, Grand Rapids, MI. Used by permission of the publisher. All rights reserved.)

Like many people, I found that God has a way of interrupting the things that we consider most important. For example, my wife and I spent years thinking and dreaming about buying a small amount of acreage back in Idaho where we could hobby farm. This led to driving hundreds of miles of county roads in southwest Idaho, considering offers and abandoning them until after several years finally finding the land we deemed perfect for our plans.

So far, so good. This soon developed into an interest in making the land a small agricultural business. We took a class to further our knowledge in how to do this. We began the process of planning, designing, and securing bids for a house (yes, our "dream house") that would become our base of operations. Then life happened, as they say.

The ordinary ups and downs of economies are nothing new in human history. I believe God uses them to fulfill His plans and draw people to trust in Him alone. They affect us individually to varying degrees and the pain can numb us to the simple fact that others are enduring pain too. The economic depression of 2009 to 2011 started with job loss that forced us to cancel our building plans. This misfortune brought about a landslide of feelings and fears I had never experienced before. At this point in life, it was like entering the mouth of a dark tunnel. In another sense it was like a house of mirrors where you see all sides of yourself with all your faults and failings . . . none of the good stuff, just the bad.

The funny thing is that I then allowed the enemy to parade all the events of my adult life before me where I had problems and failings in plain view of my peers. He made me recall several years earlier when I was working through the problems of a project that didn't come together well in construction and for which I faced heavy criticism, a project where I relied on the teamwork of others who I found had let me down and faced no repercussions, even in some sense being regarded as heroes. It was one of the political hazards of a project manager's job. You are responsible for the outcomes no matter the assurances of your team members that things are going according to plan. Under the glaring spotlight of management, I confided my troubles to another Christian man. To my surprise, his response was one of derision, even saying, "When they pay you the kind of money you make, they expect you to do your job!" The words seemed harsh at the time, but later I remembered that he had been through a devastating career setback of his own only a few years prior and in similar circumstances. Still, those words stuck in my soul like a knife and came back many times to haunt me.

David faced this kind of humbling turn in his life as his kingdom was being taken by his own son, Absalom, in a coup. It is true that David brought it on himself in midlife by his own lack of self-discipline in the moral failing with Bathsheba followed by complicity in the death of Uriah. From this, God warned David that he would face trouble from his own house and the ensuing years read like a soap opera, if it were not so tragic. As we know from our own country's experience during the Clinton presidency, it is never "just about sex." David's indiscretion led to Amnon's rationalizing the rape of Tamar, his half-sister, but Absalom's full sister. David's tepid response to this incident resulted in a loss of respect within his household. This led to Amnon's eventual murder at the hands of Absalom. Now put yourself in David's place to see if you could face such a humbling and keep on going.

In his flight from Absalom, perhaps a day's journey from Jerusalem, he is met by an insignificant little man, Shimei, who takes up a taunt and publicly shames David. In fact, he was animated about it, throwing rocks and shouting invectives that, were we to translate them into the modern vernacular, would make you blush at the coarse language. I don't particularly like paraphrases of the Scripture, but this one is good:

> *Get lost, get lost, you butcher, you hellhound! God has paid you back for all your dirty work in the family of Saul and for stealing his kingdom. God has given the kingdom to your son Absalom. Look at you now—ruined! And good riddance, you pathetic old man!* (2 Samuel 16:8, MSG, The Bible in Contemporary Language, Navpress, 2002).

Well now, that's a mouthful of criticism! The thing about criticism is it can be a good thing when given with intent to help someone improve their performance. Solomon advises this many times such as:

> *Whoever loves instruction, loves knowledge, But he who hates correction is stupid.* (Proverbs 12:1)

But it's often done with at least a little malice (and in the case of Shimei, a lot of malice), to cut someone down a few notches. What comes out is not always truthful. Shimei mixed in some lies. David had seen his measure of bloodshed as a warrior king, true enough, but he did not usurp the throne of Saul. The Lord had given the kingdom to David long before he ascended to the throne. And he was nothing but kind and forbearing to Saul when all he wanted to do was kill David. And let's not forget David's friendship with Jonathan, Saul's son.

But what I find most interesting is David's response to all of this when one of the few mighty men still loyal to him offered to sever the head of Shimei for his insolence.

> *So let him curse, because the LORD has said to him, 'Curse David.' . . . Let him alone and let him curse; for so the LORD has ordered him.* (2 Samuel 16:10, 11)

These are the words of a man who has been humbled by life. Do I really believe that the Lord ordered Shimei to say these things? Well, God can make a donkey speak, so He can certainly ordain this. David was broken enough to perceive that this could be the Lord's hand. So, when we face the harshest words, which sometimes seem to come 'out of the blue,' do we respond in like manner and acknowledge the Lord's hand in humbling us in the process of breaking us? Delivered by human tongues, it is sometimes crueler than it ought to be but can be used by God anyway.

Admittedly, my mistake was allowing the enemy to get into my head and accuse me. His pointed message? YOU REALLY ARE A FAILURE AND YOUR LIFE PROVES IT! One night as I lay in bed unable to sleep, the enemy constructed a clever narrative, and it went something like this:

> "Look at you! This is now the third time you have been unemployed. Has this happened to anyone else in your family? Look at the successful lives of others in yours and your wife's family. They don't get into this kind of trouble. Look back . . . way back. Think about those who did not respect you. And what about your children? They are not well established in life. You put them through college only

to see them in jobs that barely pay the bills. That's your fault, too."

But words on a page cannot fully describe the despair I was being dragged into that sleepless night because the mind tries to block out bad memories. To anyone else reading this, it would be difficult to understand the desert journey without some sense of what led me there. The enemy of our souls delights in attacks that interrupt our sleep. Sometimes for hours into the night, he made me stare into the dark recesses of my mind, dredging up past mistakes until I said, "It's really true! It's all true! God . . . I know you don't want me to listen to the enemy, but I think he is right!" Months down the road, he did it again after I had tried unsuccessfully to find work, interviewing several times, even as a finalist out of 50 applicants for what would have been my new dream job as a facilities department manager at a local college. "There, you see . . . nobody wants you. Too many flaws. They don't like you." And when these events cascade in a man's life, his confidence erodes. It generates palpable fear when this happens. Your self-worth is drained and makes you think that you are unhappy with the way the world has treated you. At this point, I didn't just smell the desert, I knew I was in it and surrounded by the howling jackals of the evil one trying to destroy me. My heart was breaking because I thought the desert was the last stop for a man—a place you didn't want to be.

Here is a good place to say something about fear. I have been alone in the wilderness on several occasions, mostly because no friends or family were available with whom to share the experience. On these treks, I ignored the backcountry rule that you never go alone, especially if you are hiking off the trail at some point. In those situations if you turn an ankle or worse, fall and break something, you may never be found even with the biggest search effort. In those situations, if you don't keep your wits, fear will take over. Walking alone in the quiet of the forest, I have heard imaginary voices behind me. No one was there. I got a whiff of fear whenever a tree creaked in the wind or a twig snapped in the distance and made me think a surprise waited around the next bend in the trail perhaps taking the form of a bear or mountain lion. Never happened to me though.

Real fear doesn't take physical form. Most often, it doesn't even present itself as a threat to bodily harm. In those situations, your body takes over and a rush of adrenaline puts you in survival mode quickly. No, fear is a thing of the psyche. It stalks you like a hungry, wild animal thereby robbing you of peace. It seeks to enslave you by degree. Real fear paralyzes when you realize you are staring at the unknown. It tricks you into thinking there is no way out of your dilemma. You have come to the end of your resources.

I was at the point of experiencing what real fear feels like. Now I could smell the dry, dusty wind of the desert approaching in my life.

And this was the beginning of my journey into the desert. I say beginning because you don't fully realize you are in the desert of life until things and events cascade one after the other, and you are battling one trial after another. It isn't like a desert flash flood where it all comes at once and is over. I realized I was not alone, though it seemed that way at times. Most people don't go into the wilderness to live for a while. It isn't something we choose to do. We would rather avoid it because it is hard to survive there for a long time without going in prepared. It takes a mindset and greater patience than I've got. But in my unprepared state, God began to show me things in His Word that were not understood by me before. It is in times like these that you either embrace God's Word as truth to live by or you reject His Word and go it alone.

Now years later, the enemy still creeps around to my flank. I can see him with some spiritual peripheral vision. And he is always up to the same old tactic of trying to terrorize me with thoughts of impending failure. So beware this front in the desert war. Take note of David's words in perhaps a similar time of his life:

For the enemy has persecuted my soul; he has crushed my life to the ground; he has made me dwell in darkness, like those who have long been dead. Therefore, my spirit is overwhelmed within me; my heart within me is distressed. (Psalm 143:3,4)

I still sometimes say to myself that the enemy is right; not to discredit God, but because that is how deep the lie has sunk into my being. I have not been fully convinced to root it out of my life, so the enemy just keeps using it over and over. On the one hand, the hard truth is that we are much worse than we think. On the other is the stronger fact that we have an advocate with the Father—Jesus Christ the righteous (1 John 2:1). He is our attorney, in a manner of speaking. When the enemy accuses me of not measuring up, it is soul satisfying delight to just tell him, "Go, and see my lawyer. His name is Jesus, and He will defend me against your claims."

Your first reaction to all of this might be to reason why the devil is wrong. It is a vain attempt to make yourself feel better. This is the time to pray for help and put on the armor of God. Your sleep will be better knowing you have the breastplate of righteousness—not yours, but the righteousness of Christ, the only righteousness strong enough to protect our hearts. And the helmet of salvation will keep the enemy from getting into our heads. The shield of faith will stop his flaming darts of accusation. In fact, the Bible speaks many times of our God as a shield (see Psalm 3:3 and 84:11).

And last, but not least, the sword of the Spirit. Near the end of Jesus' forty days in the desert, Satan's first temptation led to the declaration,

It is written, 'Man shall not live by bread alone, but by every word of God.' (Luke 4:4)

This is either true or it isn't. There is no middle ground. Jesus was quoting Deuteronomy 8:3 which explains why God allowed the children of Israel to suffer privation in the desert—to draw them to Him and His living Word. Even the New Testament Hebrew converts were reminded of that:

> *The word of God is living and powerful . . . and is a*
> *discerner of the thoughts and intents of the heart.*
> (Hebrews 4:12)

The word "discerner" is from *kritikos*, showing us that the Word of God is a <u>critic</u> of our very thoughts. He knows us to our core because we are made in His image. Furthermore, in the Bible, God reveals Himself to us. No other ancient literature tells of a creator who intervenes in the history of men, yet also is so personal that we can know Him on that level. One thing is certain . . . in the desert, you have nobody except God. Oh, for sure there are the trappings of life still around you and perhaps a companion, but none of those things will give your soul satisfaction like relationship to God Himself.

When life becomes dry, God's Word becomes an oasis that refreshes and nourishes our souls. In life's valleys when your mind is brought low by all that the world has turned into, Psalm 42 is helpful. First, there is the acknowledgment of our soul's unsettled times brought on by life's turbulence and things we really have no control over as individuals. We just look for a friendly face, a smile. So, the psalmist says,

> *I shall praise Him for the help of His countenance.*
> (Psalm 42:5)

There is comfort in seeing a face lit up by a genuine smile; God says, "Look at My face and that will help your blues to depart." His "smile" is the best to cheer us up.

I began to see the parallels of the wandering children of Israel in Sinai to my life. I believe now that God wants His children in every age to see this by one journey or another of His choosing. It's not the same journey for everyone. For me, it was a testing of my faith on a level that, at times, made me think it would not survive, at least as it relates to the church. Sure, I doubted the attributes of God one by one: His goodness, His faithfulness, certainly His justice. His love? Well, let's just say, it was hard to see it without understanding true agape does not mean getting things our way.

Part of being in the desert is learning who God really is. Those Sunday School truths about His nature are put to the test. What about His goodness? Did you know this doesn't mean He is about doing good for you? It means that He is not evil. He doesn't do evil. There isn't any evil around Him. Does He allow evil to happen? Yes. But when bad things happen to us, when people hurt us or do wicked things, God is still good. It is part of who He is. Understanding this will help you travel the desert well.

CHAPTER 2

TRAVELING LIFE'S DESERTS

We all conjure many questions when in the desert of life. Of course, the first are probably, "Why?" and "Why me?" "What is God up to?" Also, "Who am I now?" Or, related to that, "Will things return to normal?" These are typical human thoughts born out of fear for the inhospitable nature of a desert experience. Oh sure, we don't mind a brief excursion. That doesn't scare us. Remember, though, that even God doesn't want to waste time. Sometimes in our frantic desire to get out of the trouble spots, we hurry when God says, "Wait on me; I have a lesson to teach here."

For me, occasional sandstorms were blowing across the barren landscape. My wife, too, felt the hot desert sand under her feet, the absence of friends and the uncertainty of what lay ahead. I remember many times during this perplexing period of our lives she would say, "I just want this to be over!" In that, she spoke from her heart what I thought many times—that we want an end point established where we get off the scorching sand and back to normal life.

This experience brought to mind the question, just what is essential for the desert traveler's journey? In this chapter, I propose a few things that might be important.

Encouragement

When I lost employment, we noticed that friends in the body of Christ would only talk to us about my joblessness. It was good that they were concerned and told us they were praying. But one thing we came to understand is that people are not one-dimensional. During a crisis, they are still in need of social contact, love, and acceptance. And when that is missing, you begin to wonder what you have done wrong. A sense of guilt or even shame that may not be warranted comes along with the feeling that we might not be socially acceptable anymore. This kind of thing makes you feel more like circumstances are your fault. The feeling of shame comes from thinking that you have been banished. It isn't true, but you think it is.

God may deal differently with your spouse than He does with you because He probably has a different way to his or her heart. I have been tempted many times to think that my wife was an innocent victim of my own troubles, that she didn't deserve this. It certainly wasn't her fault. Sometimes, it isn't a matter of fault at all because when God wants to get our attention, what better way than to bring some discomfort or pain into our lives. I was bitter enough at times to keep God's Word from acting on me. I learned that bitterness is a harsh task master. In fact, God made me confront that sin often during the desert experience because I was so focused on what harm other people had done to me. To be honest, it's a sin with which I still struggle.

I have learned through this experience that it can hollow out a marriage if couples don't open their hearts to one another and express their feelings of loss, hurt and shame. For wives, my advice would be to verbally encourage your husband from time to time by telling him the things he has done right and the dreams he has are still worth pursuing. Don't let your pride get in the way of doing that. You must realize that it is difficult for a man to express his feelings of brokenness. His ego is driven by the desire to be successful and to provide for his family. When those things aren't happening, even for a season such as this desert brings, it is daunting to him. Husbands, your wife probably needs to be reassured that she will get through what seems to be a bleak time of desolation. Make sure you don't withhold what the other needs. But for both men and women in the desert, the way they are treated by other people (maybe ostracism or even being forgotten for a long season) tends to make them think that these are things God is using to confirm His displeasure; that God somehow speaks through the words and actions of mere people . . . even though this is not, in truth, how God acts.

Talking With God

This whole matter of prayer is taken for granted in the Christian's life. It is simple in concept yet there is mystery in how it works. I say that a person in the desert of life should not be reticent in asking for prayer from others because it can become like an oasis—cool and refreshing while renewing hope. Still, most of us would admit we don't know why God needs to hear from more than just one person about a particular need. We learn from the Sermon on the Mount that He knows what we need before we ask, so why request others to join in praying for us? I can only offer a few ideas here. I have heard it said that when we pray, humanity is cooperating with God. That sounds good, but still leaves me searching for more meaning to the subject. The fundamental thing about prayer is relationship. Without prayer, how can you have a vibrant, growing relationship with your creator? I like the way Ray Stedman used the example of a marriage without regularly hearing the voice of your spouse:

> "Everyone knows of couples that have stopped speaking to each other. Such a marriage is a disintegrating union, a dead relationship. Human desires and needs require speech; they

must be expressed; there must be interchange—a flow of words for a marriage to be a live, fruitful, vital relationship. Prayer also is an absolute necessity in the interchange of a child's heart with the Father." (*Talking to My Father*, Ray Stedman, Our Daily Bread Publishing, fair use granted)

Part of what we accomplish when we invite others to pray for us in a matter is bringing *them* into closer relationship with God. Too often, I think, people grow weary in the type of prayer that the desert dweller needs. It is usually a long season of life, so don't be bashful about reminding your prayer partners from time to time of your need. Help them to know where your heart is at, even if it is just a need for greater discernment about God's will. In that way, not only are they growing in relationship with God, they are also gaining the heart of God in sympathizing with your situation in life. When we give up praying for someone's long dry season, our hearts grow cold and cynical. We may start to think things like, "Why can't that person find a job?" Or, "Isn't it a pity that her children don't speak with her anymore?"

The type of prayer you are asking them to engage in is called supplication. In the New Testament, there is one Greek word almost always translated into English this way. Paul used it in Ephesians 6:18 along with the admonition to *persevere*. It is a petition, but the root word means 'to beg.' Viewed that way, it is not a passive activity but one of importunity. We know from the parable of the unjust judge that God is eager to answer us (more on this later). But answers don't come until we ask. It makes our faith stronger and encourages us to trust God more when we see him answer prayer. And when we are persevering in prayer, we are always on the lookout for His answers. Jesus drives this point home when following the parable with the question,

Nevertheless, when the Son of Man comes, will He really find faith on the earth? (Luke 18:8)

Our faith becomes evident when we trust God enough to pray and seek His face, yes, this divine being that we cannot see with our eyes while dwelling on earth.

Healing

Another thing we bring about when we ask others to pray is our own healing.

> *Confess your trespasses to one another, and pray for one another, that you may be healed. The effective, fervent prayer of a righteous man avails much.* (James 5:16)

Note that the prayer you are requesting is fervent . . . it is not passive. When I was a young man, I was taught this verse applied to physical healing. A closer look shows something more wonderful. For 'trespasses' here, most contemporary English translations use 'sin.' It is best to understand sin as "missing the mark" (like a marksman missing the bullseye on the target) and this is how the word is translated in the majority of New Testament uses. In this one instance, however, the word is *paratugehano*. It means those things that come along, beginning with the familiar prefix *para* which we use in English for such words now as paralegal (one who works alongside an attorney providing things like research, but does not have a license to practice law). It literally means those occurrences that come with life; those things that happen to us, whether sickness or trial or loss or anguish. The word for healed means to be cured either in a literal or figurative sense. Even in the trials and troubles of life, we need the curing hand of Jesus to touch us.

But let's not leave this thought without some application to ours and others' lives. If we are honest, the first inclination most of us have toward others who fall into trouble or trial of one kind or another is to shrink back. We might be subconsciously saying that we don't want to get involved in someone else's pain or, worse, that we might wonder if their trouble is like a disease that, if we got too close, others might see and judge us. In other words, we tend to at least isolate the sufferer in the body of Christ, leaving them alone when they need help the most. We might just be afraid to get involved. In this passage, James is admonishing us to get past all of that and get involved in helping others to wellness and wholeness. If you see that someone is suffering the kind of isolation brought on by the desert in their lives, don't shrink back; come alongside them. Are they in some legal trouble? Are they stuck in chronic unemployment? Has their family abandoned them? Are they hurting over the loss of a beloved friend or pet? Is there a crisis going on in their lives? Don't err on the side of caution. Rather, err on the side of love by going to them with physical presence and prayer. The problem isn't that people have enough friends, but that we all have too few genuine friendships. Without sounding laborious, I don't think the point can be made much clearer.

Judge Not

Since we have been talking about how best to help the desert traveler in prayer, allow me to interject here some lessons on judging others because the person in a desert struggle often is self-conscious from the feeling that he/she is being judged in some way. I was confused about this matter as a result of our cultural acceptance of the notion that we are not to judge another person. Because Jesus said in the Sermon,

Judge not, that you be not judged, (Matthew 7:1)

even the world has twisted it to mean something entirely different. In the vernacular, it means don't criticize me for what I do. It is a defense mechanism often deployed to keep people away from our faults, excuse our behavior or, worse, to continue in our sins. It is our nature to make judgments about things and people. When we make private pronouncements about public personalities with whom we have no personal acquaintance, we are simply expressing an opinion and not really hurting anyone. As Christians, we should never be coarse and demeaning, but we are also not being judgmental when we offer advice or counsel to other Christians who may be blind to faults or actions that can hurt them or the testimony of Christ. In other words, we don't ignore what is wrong, but we also don't criticize unfairly or unjustly. Otherwise, we are playing God.

John Stott defines the biblical sense of judging as that which puts the worst possible spin on others' *motives*. This might be revealed as pouring cold water on other peoples' schemes or making an example of others' mistakes. In Matthew 7:1 the word is used figuratively of a magistrate handing down a sentence (judge = *krino*). To be sure, most of our judging is silent. It is as if one is making a judicial condemnation, but it is done mentally. Even if you haven't said anything, our Lord sets a higher standard in the kingdom sermon. When making a mental judgment about someone, the problem arises if our motive is wrong; that is, if we are plainly trying to find fault in someone. We sinners have a strong propensity for that. It is helpful, I think, to always start with the questions: Would I really act any differently than them? Does my hypocrisy show by my own past behavior? Jesus expands on this in Matthew 7:3, admonishing us to get the beam out of our eye first.

Job's friends were on the right track for the first week of their visit after all the calamity occurred in his life. They sat in silence. Then do you remember what happened? Each one began to find fault. They used errant theological arguments and personal opinions to explain why he was suffering. They provide us with examples of what it means to judge someone. They had passed judgment based on what they thought.

When I worked for a soda ash producer in Wyoming in the mid-1990s (most people ask what it is—a chemical used primarily in the manufacture of glass), I received an assignment to shepherd the design and construction of a large addition to the conveying capacity of the plant's railcar loading facility. The budget was $4.5 million and included coordination of work from four separate engineering consulting firms as well as several of my department colleagues. The schedule was tight and made even more so by being put at the end of the line by management who had more power over construction resources for their related projects. That was compounded by the hiring of a new engineering department manager, a non-engineer without experience and who was antagonistic to nearly all in the department. From a career standpoint, it was the first large-scale project entrusted to me by my previous boss who was probably the best of any that I had. The stakes were high. It was gut-grinding work. In the end, most of the objectives were met with time to spare.

Even with this measured success, I was given a poor performance review (by now, from yet another new boss who was not involved in the department and replacing the other after only nine months). I learned from this how perceptions play into corporate politics. At the same time, a co-worker was receiving similar treatment. We both learned that we were singled out by management because we were easy targets. Others with only support roles in my project received better reviews and moved ahead in their careers while I was left without a reasonable path forward. Though it was tough to take at the time, it is illustrative. Most of us know what it means to suffer the "slings and arrows of outrageous fortune." But we cannot always control what others think of us.

We might be performing at our zenith and still be undercut by those who have a bad opinion of us or are jealous. They might even feel threatened by us and what we represent. All of us are guilty of it at one time or another. My limited research did not yield a satisfying definition for the saying, "perception is reality" so I will offer this: it means your judgments about a person's character, abilities, or personality guide your actions toward them. It is quite lazy of people to think this way. It doesn't take into consideration all that is going on in the individual's life or all the effects of others' actions that affect an outcome. In the business world, you are not cut that kind of slack, but it ought not to be that way among believers in Jesus. One of its outgrowths is "jumping to conclusions" regarding people about whom we actually know very little. It only works in the realm of so-called magic acts where the illusionist makes you believe that what he is doing really happened, though it was not possible by all the physical laws of nature.

When you are married to a person for more than a few years, perceptions about them fall away as you get to know them and learn what it means to love. The Word of God instructs us to be discerning. Discerning of spirits is even a special ability conferred by the Holy Spirit. But it is not the same as perception. Discerning requires engagement of the mental faculties and senses that God gave us. When we let perception guide us, we start treating people with contempt and even try to manipulate the relationship. It fosters a breakdown in human relationships.

When you come to the realization that you can't stop what people think or say about you, it is helpful to understand what Paul writes:

> *But he who is spiritual judges all things, yet he himself is rightly judged by no one.* (1 Corinthians 2:15)

Here a prefix is added to the word 'judge' (*anakrino*) to denote an intense investigation by the person who is led by the Holy Spirit. In the word's legal sense, it is an extensive study of the evidence in a case. The last half of the verse could mean that people of the world system don't understand the person who is devoted to Christ. I learn from this verse that we are to focus our minds on understanding all things of the Spirit and not worry what other people think about us.

It is extremely difficult to escape the trap of caring what others think of us, but very liberating when we do.

When is it wrong to judge someone? On a practical level, I found the following advice to be helpful:
- When you are angry or emotionally involved
- You have a desire to punish or get even
- There is envy or jealousy in your heart
- People say something you don't like
- Your self-esteem is the matter

Also, this is a simple acrostic for NEED when we are dealing with people:

Necessary – to say this?
Encourage – will it?
Edify – will it?
Dignify – will it show respect for the person?

Sensing God's Presence

Even in the bleakest of times when nothing seems to be going your way and a sense of emptiness pervades, you need to look for God's hand—whether as the loving heavenly Father or His representation in Christ or the comfort of the Holy Spirit. He will act on your behalf to make Himself known in this time, but you also must be aware of and obedient to His call even when you don't feel like it.

To illustrate, our family hiked across the Grand Canyon in late May of 2000. It was an epic adventure and I learned many things from this vacation. Most people visiting Grand Canyon National Park are there for the magnificent view from the top. Few people do the trek from rim to rim. It was something we wanted to do ever since visiting there a few years prior when our children were still very young. We longed to give them this experience for a lasting memory and, indeed, they have not forgotten it because of the hardship they endured (though I think their memories of it are mostly fond now). Even my lovely wife did it . . . with a pack on her back. You must prepare physically and secure permits months in advance for the limited camping sites in the canyon. In the weeks before our adventure, we prepared our bodies by hiking the desert canyon north of our house, gradually increasing our mileage to build endurance. We already lived at a high elevation in Green River, Wyoming so didn't need much acclimation to oxygen deprivation at the similar elevation of the canyon rims. We even learned on this trip that there are people who organize an extraordinary event to run from the south rim to the north—just short of an actual marathon. Some even hike from rim to rim and back in one day!

Now the Grand Canyon is desert landscape for sure, though there are occasional rushing streams of water that seem to appear out of nowhere from the canyon walls. Still, you go for long stretches without water to fill your bottles. Believe it or not, this is a desert adventure where you learn that you are surrounded by perils otherwise largely ignored. You aren't overwhelmed by them because you have a plan of attack. Nonetheless, they are there. Our plan included parking our car at the south rim, taking a shuttle van ride to the north rim (200 miles) and camping there the night before our trek into the canyon. At this time, our son was 17 and our daughter, 14. The north rim of the canyon is 8240 feet above sea level. It was near freezing when we awoke at dawn, scarfed a quick breakfast, and began our 16-mile, 6000 foot descent to Phantom Ranch at the canyon bottom. Yes, we had to make it all that way by nightfall.

In the canyon that day, temperatures were in the 90's. About halfway down from the north rim, we were in the heat of the day. . . no shade to be found. I could tell that the trek was beginning to take its toll on our daughter—physically and mentally. She was always game for adventure, but half the battle for anyone in the wilderness is mental. Your body can take a lot of punishment as long as your mind tells it to keep going. Marathoners will testify of that.

A spring from the wall of Grand Canyon
(Photo credit: author)

My daughter began to complain. Mind you, she was young then and the hike was grueling by that time. Our packs were too heavy with equipment I realized later we should never have taken (my fault). Even I began to worry. We still had a long way to go. She began to slow down to a pace that I knew was dangerous because it only kept us in the hot sun longer until we reached the next watering hole. She was falling behind and getting separated from the rest of us. I recall the need to get her mind right, an unpleasant duty that a father must do from time-to-time, knowing it is for the good of his children. So, I gave up on patiently urging her on and just told her to stop complaining and move! I sensed that if she gave up, we would be in trouble and not reach our destination by nightfall. To her credit, she responded. Together, we finally arrived at the campsite an hour after sunset (nearly 11 p.m.), groping in the dark and collapsing exhausted on the picnic tables there. I felt like an ogre having put my family through that, but we knew it would be a difficult day.

I think we all learned some things from the experience, not the least of which was our love for one another revealed in toughness and tender moments. As my wife and children lay there that night unable to move another inch, I put cookies in their mouths like a mother bird feeding her young. We were at the end of ourselves, physically, but stuck together because of our commitment to each other. My point of application here is simply that the desert will drive us to exhaustion if we do not trust our heavenly Father. We might even find ourselves stranded if we don't heed the urgings of the Holy Spirit.

The hike out of the canyon also gave me something to recall God's presence. After resting a full day, we had to hike nine miles and rise 4000 feet in elevation from the Colorado River to the South Rim where we had reserved a comfortable motel bed. The most we had ever done on previous hikes was five miles and 1500 feet elevation rise. We started before sunrise, knowing that we would need many rests along the way, especially as the day got warmer. We crossed the footbridge over the river at sunrise and headed confidently up the trail. There were many other people hiking that day and we tried to pace ourselves, perhaps resting longer than we should have in the heat of the day. But as nightfall approached, we were still about a half mile from the trailhead at the canyon top. We were alone, exhausted, very hungry, and out of water. At this point, the trail is narrow with drop-offs not friendly to an errant hiker, especially in the dark. We had flashlights, but they were small pen lights that were practically useless to a hiker. We rounded a bend in the trail and took a rest break. Looking at the number of switchbacks ahead of us, I was starting to get a little nervous, though not letting my family know.

It was dark now . . . about 11 p.m. with the stars out. As we sat there munching on some trail mix, a small group of men (from India, as it appeared to me) approached from the trail below and stopped to rest with us. They had big flashlights. If you think about it, they didn't need to stop. They could have just gone up the trail. Instead, they invited us to follow them. I remember making the remark to them that they could be guardian angels, even if they would not admit it. One of them just smiled back. We followed them up to the top for the next half hour. When we got there, no sooner had we taken our packs off, than we turned around and they were nowhere to be seen. It was as if they had vanished into thin air. To this day, I believe God had sent some angels just for us. So great was His care and concern for our safe arrival at midnight on the south rim of the Grand Canyon. It is a treasured memory of mine.

In the same way, if you don't believe that He wants to show Himself to you in the desert of life, you are missing a very important part of the journey. It is part of experiencing God, His wonder and His provision. Remembering what God has already done will help keep you going. Look in Psalm 77 for a lesson about this. The writer says when we think God has forgotten us, we need to remember what He has done in the ancient past (vs. 5), not just what He is doing for us today. That word has the general meaning of time out-of-mind. That is why we have the Bible, to think about His works of creation and the mighty acts like redeeming His people from Egypt. If you forget about self-awareness and focus on what He wants to show you about Himself, your desert journey will make you stronger.

Just as the wilderness is a place where you are far from worldly influences, the desert days of life can be a time that you focus your mind on God (Romans 12:2). You can pray a lot and meditate on Scripture as you walk down the dusty trail. I think this is mostly what God had in mind for the soon-to-be nation of Israel. No doubt, after 400 years of bondage in Egypt, Israel had been strongly influenced by Egyptian culture. They needed to learn the discipline of worship and just who exactly Yahweh is and how to love Him in accordance with the first commandment. But you need to be away from worldly influences to learn that. It is the nature of this world system to pull us away from allegiance to God.

And when you first head into the realities of the wilderness experience in your life, you pine for the good ol' days like the children of Israel did in wanting to go back to their gardens. Had they forgotten already how bad their slavery was at the hands of Pharaoh—a living personification of the world system? I recall even on our recreational trips to the wilderness how, from the first day, myself as a young man and even later, my children, would think about what they missed most at home—the better food, better drink (soda is too heavy to pack). My dad would even plan to leave a six pack of pop in the creek nearest the car plus a hearty snack or can of beef stew in the trunk for our return . . . so we would have something of the 'luxuries' of life to look forward to and talk about in the middle of the sometimes arduous trek. Oh, we look forward to an adventure, but we certainly don't want to stay there. The vacation has a planned beginning and end, but not so in the desert with God. The journey is done when He has completed his work. That is unsettling to us because we know that the desert is not a place where we are intended to get comfortable.

I recently heard that in hard times, it is not wrong to ask the Lord why it is happening, but that it is wrong to ask, "Why me?" I think there is truth to that. In fact, the proper attitude should confidently say, "Why not me?" Sometimes the first thought in times of trial is that in some way we have displeased God (never mind that we cannot put our finger on it exactly). What about, when in the desert where you believe God wants you to know Him better, you get the feeling He is NOT there with you? Isn't it reasonable to expect that we can experience His presence even in these desolate times? What if He doesn't SEEM to be nearby? If only we could have the pillar of cloud and fire manifestation of God like Israel did in their journey through Sinai, most of us would be ecstatic! We can only imagine what that must have been like, a constant reminder of God's presence. Now, we have God's Word as a reminder of His presence.

We also need to rehearse truth, especially in those hard times or when we think God doesn't care. That is, our habit should always be to remember what God has said, not what we think or feel about God. In fact, our feelings may run opposite to that. We need to remember just who God is, what He has said about Himself. We must steel our resolve that His Word is the well we draw from to satisfy a thirsty soul. We must not be deceived by the enemy into thinking it is all about feeling His presence.

We also must not neglect worship—in church for sure, but also in our private times with God. I find myself to be deficient not only in the concept of worship, but worshiping God in the deep valleys of life. We all struggle with that because we cannot get past our self-pity, but it's also because of our misunderstanding of revealed truth about God and His purpose for trial and suffering. Take a minute to think about the situation in which Paul and Silas found themselves after casting out a demon from a girl. The hubbub that followed resulted in their imprisonment (Acts 16)! Has that ever happened to us? For most people, the answer is no. What was their response to such injustice? It was worship and praise that turned the heads of those in their presence and resulted in conversions of their jailors to faith in Christ. But remember, rehearsing truth is a discipline of the spirit.

CHAPTER 3

THE TRAIL OF TRIALS

I call the desert of our days a trial—a time of suffering. It can be a hard journey. Many things have been written on the biblical basis for suffering. Here, I offer a different perspective after my own look into the mirror of God's Word (James 1:24) and meditating on some of the words used by New Testament authors. Think of it here as the amateur theologian's observations and a practical guide on what Scripture says about suffering.

Here in America we do not understand real suffering for the faith, although it is beginning to occur with legal challenges to our freedom of conscience and practice. But that does not take away from our shared experience with all humanity of trial and trouble. Even persecution takes many forms, some so subtle they creep up and nibble on the faithful like bedbugs in the night.

Earlier, I stipulated that we should ask the question, "why not me?" when experiencing difficulties in life. In this chapter, let's explore a corollary to that. To what end are my sufferings? That is, what is their purpose?

The book of Job is among the oldest in the Bible and perhaps even among all literature. And what is its central theme? Suffering and pain. Now, it's true that Job devolves into some doubt and questioning of God concerning his pain and loss. His rants are exacerbated by his friends' words. He is, after all, only human, and we all have had the same response in unwelcome times of trouble. In the end, God's answer to him can be distilled to this tenet for our benefit as well – men do not know and cannot know everything. God who created the universe should be acknowledged as The Almighty no matter what we think. Figuring out the cause of our trials and pain is often counter-productive from God's perspective.

We shy away from suffering as a rule, because we can do nothing about it. Suffering has the power to incapacitate or at least slow us down. And we don't like that. After all, God's kingdom doesn't advance much when we are struck with a blow? Doesn't seem like the most efficient way to get things done, does it? But there are some eye-opening lessons about suffering that you simply cannot understand without a baptism in the experience. They are lessons at which the soul cringes because when you are confronted with your inadequacies, weaknesses, and utter helplessness, you are stripped bare.

I don't pretend to be a scholar of New Testament Greek, but it is fun to discover that many of our English words have their origins in the Greek. These words, or parts of words, with which we are familiar take on an exciting dimension when we see how God links them through the centuries to our time. In this portion of the book, I want to delve into the many descriptions of suffering in the New Testament where, in most cases, there are just one or two English words used. I think it helps to know how the writers saw suffering with different facets and that their view applies just the same now as it did in the days of the early church. In other words, suffering isn't just persecution. Everyone suffers at times throughout life, not just those who follow Jesus.

On the Open Sea

Peter, James, and Paul deal with the subject of suffering in their letters to the church. I'll start with James' letter to Israeli Christians in exile. Though we often view chapter 1 as a compilation of themes on trials, prayer and temptation, there is really a central theme of suffering that runs through the chapter. The latter part deals with the importance of rehearsing truth in the midst of trial because that is how you get through it.

James (the half-brother of Jesus) begins his epistle by saying our response to trials should be joy. Our natural reaction to a statement like that is mostly, "How can you be joyous in difficult circumstances?" We just want to find a way out of them as soon as possible so we don't experience shame before our friends and enemies. Here, James introduces the discipline of <u>choosing</u> joy . . . as a volitional act. He says,

> *My brethren, count it all joy when you <u>fall into</u> various trials,* (James 1:2)

The underlined words come from one word in the original - *peripipto*. We use the prefix *peri* in words like periscope and perimeter. In the latter case, we are usually talking about the boundary of a circle or the fence line of a corral; you get the idea. Think of yourself somewhere inside that circle and the literal sense is to <u>be surrounded</u>.

The word for trials here (*peirasmos*) sounds familiar linguistically and is interesting for the fact that its roots have to do with a test by way of piercing (*peira* in Hebrews 11:36). At the very least, there is implied adversity. The use of military terminology here should get our attention. When James wrote this to the scattered church (vs. 2), Christians were facing what we would consider unbelievable hardship through persecution and being literally forced into exile at the edge of a sword. Some think this is because of the pre-conversion persecutions instigated by Saul since the epistle of James is perhaps the earliest of all New Testament writings. Saints today in that part of the world are still experiencing the trials of exile and much worse, even the kind of suffering you would only attach to the end times. An example is the persecution of Christians in Syria and Iraq by ISIS beginning around 2010.

Not to cheapen that, but aren't we who are in the desert of life surrounded by trials at times, as if an army were around us on all flanks with their sharpened swords and spears ready to pierce the bubble of our lives or our dreams? And James writes "count it all joy?" The word for joy here is *chara*, It is calm delight. I usually protest to God when I am surrounded by circumstances outside of my control, almost like Israel in the harsh wilderness. I am not full of calm delight.

Isn't it enough that we simply believe? Why must God test our faith in him? It is largely because our faith atrophies when not tested. James is making the point here that the path of testing leads to greater patience in us (*hupomone* = stay under; "hupo" is easier to remember as the opposite of "hyper"). Patience is the unseen result of testing that helps keep our faith strong when we would otherwise doubt in times of trial.

Most of us are impatient for trials to be over, but God is after the practical ends of *teleios*, perfection, and *holoklero,* completeness (James 1:4). That might seem like lofty idealism, but it is helpful to understand the prefixes. We use *tele* in words such as telephone or telescope—the idea of looking at something far off or hearing something far away but bringing it closer through optical devices or electronics. From the prefix *holo* we get our word 'whole' so it all comes together as God's aim for us to experience trials with the calmness derived from knowing their purpose—to bring us closer to wholeness or maturity in Christ. We certainly may not know what is going to happen next or even be adequately prepared for it, but the directive from God is to be calm about it in view of the eventual outcome in our lives. Riches are mentioned here to remind that even money isn't going to deliver you from trials, so don't trust in them (James 1:10 and 11).

The Proverbs of Solomon counsel us about how gaining wisdom will help us avoid unnecessary suffering, i.e., suffering that derives from our own lack of discretion or bad behavior or bad decisions. But in the kind of suffering over which we have little to no control, James admonishes us to <u>ask</u> for wisdom (James 1:5). Then, in asking, we should not be double-minded; that is, asking on the one hand followed by doubting on the other that God will deliver (James 1:8). He emphasizes this by adding that doubting is like being on the *pelagos*, the wide, open sea. It seems such an unusual word to use here. We get our word archipelago from this, defined as an expanse of water with many scattered islands (at least it has some small areas of land on which to take refuge). The Jews of antiquity had a superstitious fear of being out on the open water, even the Sea of Galilee which, by our standards, is just a large lake. I have only been on the open ocean once, just a couple miles from shore on a small guide-fishing boat. It rocked and pitched on normal wave action, no storms; so much so that I got violently seasick. Being on a large ferry boat or cruise ship makes all the difference in how you handle the ride.

Another experience I had in 2004 was just at the edge of the Pacific Ocean in the Barclay Sound off Vancouver Island. My brother was piloting a motorized inflatable raft while I fished. It was fun and land was not far away in the form of the little island on which we were camped, but I got the feeling of smallness even in little swells that we were experiencing as I looked out over the vastness of the ocean beyond. I couldn't help but imagine what terror there would be if we were swept out to the open sea or overturned right there.

Reading the story of Ernest Shackleton's incredible survival on an Antarctic expedition (the book is called *Endurance*, and it was required reading for our children), you can't help being amazed how he and several other crew members sailed 800 miles from Elephant Island through gale-force winds and incredibly high seas in a life boat, navigating under the worst imaginable conditions. After two weeks, they reached a whaling station at South Georgia Island so the remaining crew members stranded on Elephant Island could be rescued.

I learned something about the empirical science of waves when designing breakwaters and docks for marinas in Idaho's state parks. The most critical aspect of wave development is called 'fetch.' It is the unimpeded open stretch of water subject to wind before it makes landfall. The longer the fetch, the taller the waves in a storm with high winds because the wind is essentially pushing the water into a pile. When you are on the wide open ocean, the fetch stretching as far as the eye can see, the waves can be immense. My point in all these examples is that when we doubt, we are essentially helpless, like a little boat in the middle of the ocean being tossed about by wind-blown waves. When we doubt that God will answer us in the trials of life, we might as well be on the storm-tossed barrenness of the *pelagos*.

Many years ago, I sought counsel from my pastor regarding a decision to leave my job and move to the Boise area for several reasons, both personal and professional. I had recently bought land in western Idaho and thought this might be God's impetus to move us on. Talking to me about how to determine God's will, I picked up something related to times of trial. He spoke of them as being in the eye of the storm—within a hurricane. He diagrammed it as being carried by the storm either to shore (i.e. home) or out into the open sea, which he dubbed 'the peril of the offing.' The dictionary definition of offing is the part of the deep sea that is visible from shore. Figuratively, it is the foreseeable future. I think his point was that sometimes our decisions in trials are hasty and, instead of leading us to safety, lead us to the barren isolation of the open sea where there may be no rescue. The analogy isn't perfect because you can see that the life of Paul is replete with examples of decisions he had to make amid trial and persecution with outcomes less than ideal. Would we say, therefore, that his trials were not ordained of God? I think it is OK to see that God sometimes uses trials to move us on and even move us out of a place where we have become stuck in a comfort zone. But it becomes perilous when we ask for direction while doubting that God will give it.

If you make it to the safety of land, it may be the deserted island that makes you feel alone, even abandoned by God. My pastor in Wyoming was fond of quoting Vance Havner, who once said of such circumstances in life, that we are "shipwrecked on God; stranded on omnipotence." Many times that saying has brought reassurance in the desert day of my soul. H. Norman Wright's advice is helpful here as well:

> "Even though you feel adrift on the turbulent ocean, God is holding you and knows the direction of your drift. Giving yourself permission to wait can give you hope. It is all right for God to ask us to wait for weeks and months and even years." (*Recovering from Losses in Life*, H. Norman Wright, copyright 1991, republished 2006, Fleming H. Revell Co., p. 141, permission by fair use policy)

Temptation

Next, James addresses the matter of trial by temptation (James 1:12). I take this to mean more of an internal battle with evil. And James reminds us that we are blessed if we endure it (*hupomeno* = to remain under). The difficulty with these verses is that there seems to be a distinction between the trials of verse 3 and temptation in verse 12. We know from the context that God sends trials but not temptations. Most commentaries connect temptations with hardships because this verse is about enduring them. You don't endure easy times, do you? No, you enjoy them. Verse 14 in James 1 carries the thought further in explaining the progression of sin. After all, sin results from temptation. That draws me a little further along the way to understand what Jesus was saying in Matthew 6:13 regarding not being led into temptation. We know God wouldn't lead us into temptation. This verse has more to do with fighting life's spiritual battles. In other words, we are asking for Holy Spirit power to avoid or hold off the temptations that might otherwise lead to our downfall. It also might be helpful to understand it as John Calvin phrased it, "That we may not be led into temptation, deliver us from evil."

Applying this truth to our desert experiences is not difficult if we accept the fact that evil exists in this world. Any understanding of history or a daily reading of the news makes this clear. We often feel that we are surviving the desert because we are trying not to fall prey to the wild beasts and bandits that can destroy us there. Satan is called a roaring lion, seeking whom he may devour; the one who wants to steal, kill, and destroy. You know this from your own experience. Has he stolen your joy and peace? Has he destroyed the faith of your child? Has a friendship or marriage broken down? We would rather avoid these kinds of hardships. They tempt us to bitterness, unkindness, or hatred; sometimes even abandonment of our commitments to others and God. So, we must ask Him for power to endure and not be overtaken by them.

Feeling the Pain

Pascho is has the meaning of <u>experiencing</u> a painful sensation and is used in all the Gospels to describe what Jesus would go through in His passion. In the same way, Jesus told Ananias that He would show Paul how much he would have to suffer for His name. But remember the suffering of the Messiah encompassed more than just the physical pain of crucifixion. He also suffered humiliation, rejection and shame. These are certainly some of the sufferings we go through in desert times, aren't they? The same word is used exclusively in Peter's treatise on suffering, though in a more general sense because he is bringing home the point that suffering should not be thought of as a strange occurrence; rather, it is to be expected in this life and he offers help in dealing with it (more on this later).

And the letter to the Hebrew Christians is written to give hope that Jesus is sufficient for all our suffering. Therefore, don't give up on your faith in Him. Our inclination in times of hardship is to drift from the truth. The writer of this letter says it is at those times that we need to pay more attention to the Word of God (Hebrews 2:1). As the letter concludes, we read:

> *Consider* (analogidzomahee) *Him who endured such hostility from sinners against Himself, lest you become weary and discouraged.* (Hebrews 12:3)

In other words, our suffering is analogous to that of Jesus and the analogy is we are striving <u>against</u> sin. In this broken-down world, we suffer, not to experience shame but to do the same thing Paul spoke of in his letter to the church in Colossae:

> *I now rejoice in my sufferings for you, and fill up in my flesh what is lacking in the afflictions of Christ, for the sake of His body, which is the church.* (Colossians 1:24)

How can there be anything lacking in Christ's suffering? It is only in the sense that we add our suffering to it so God's story of redemption is made known through Christ's body, the Church.

Pascho is perhaps the type of suffering with which most of us so easily identify. In early 2010, my wife was experiencing some health problems that were best fixed by several procedures performed laparoscopically in the same operation. The surgeon was confident from years of experience that it would be routine with a return to work within perhaps a week. We needed her income as I had just been laid off from my job. The day of surgery arrived, and I accompanied my wife to the hospital early in the morning. A gracious pastor from the community that was volunteering his time even prayed with us. Her surgery was supposed to take perhaps an hour and a half.

As that time elapsed and stretched into two, then two and a half hours, I became anxious not having heard from the doctor. Finally, after three hours, he walked into the waiting room and began to explain complications that had arisen. They involved more invasive surgical procedures. To top it all off, he had nicked her colon, only discovering his error after deciding to double-check where he thought that might have occurred. (I think it was a guardian angel tapping him on the shoulder.) Fortunately, the surgical specialist for those kinds of repairs was there finishing up another surgery and was able to do a repair at that time. But because of that mistake, her doctor was unable to complete all the planned surgery. After five hours, my wife was in recovery and later in the afternoon awoke wondering what had happened.

What was supposed to be a one-night stay in the hospital turned into almost a week followed by another week of rest at home before returning to work, though still in a painful condition. She was working two part-time jobs and couldn't do the afternoon one for a while. Full recovery took most of the next six months just healing the incision, etc. Now I don't write this to whine . . . surgeries sometimes don't go as planned. It was a time of intense physical suffering for her, during which I felt helpless and frustrated that nothing could be done about it. This episode in our lives shows what physical pain and mental anguish we all endure from time to time.

All Together Now . . .

Just before the great love chapter in the first letter to the church at Corinth, Paul writes about suffering in the context of unity in the body.

> *And if one member suffers* (pascho)*, all the members suffer* (sumpascho) *with it.* (1 Corinthians 12:26)

With the prefix *sum,* we are talking about experiencing it together as the <u>sum</u> of all parts making the whole. We are, in effect, suffering the same thing. We know the analogy works from our own experience with physical pain. Try throwing out your back and see what effect it has on the rest of the body. Likewise, one individual member of the church experiencing pain hurts the rest of the church as well. When those hurts go unnoticed or are not ministered to by the healthy parts of the church body, we limp along more often than we should.

The same word is used to show that we also suffer with Christ:

> . . .*if indeed we suffer with Him, that we may also*
> *be glorified together.* (Romans 8:17)

How is it possible that we suffer with Jesus? It is suffering of the same kind; the unique suffering of persecution for our faith in Him.

Feeling the Pressure

The scope of suffering is further revealed in Paul's second letter to the Corinthians. He begins the letter,

> *Blessed be the God . . . who comforts us in all our*
> *tribulation . . .* (2 Corinthians 1:3 and 4)

Thlipsis is the peculiar word in the original and is used for both tribulation and trouble (NKJV). It is different from other trials because it has to do with the <u>pressures</u> we face. Vines, MacArthur, and others say that the word is used figuratively most often in the New Testament, but its original use creates the picture of pressing olives or grapes (The MacArthur New Testament Commentary, Romans 1-8, April, 1991, Moody Publishers). What is inside is now coming out and so it is with the believer in that now Christ is coming out in our times of *thlipsis*. Hence, it is always God's purpose to show Christ to the world, whether in our bold proclamation of the Gospel or in the times of affliction. Pervasive in our culture is to think, "How did you get yourself into this or that bind?" Or, "What did you do wrong?" Sometimes it has nothing to do with what we did or didn't do, only that God wants Christ to come out in our times of trouble or even in our most stressful situations.

We don't always live under pressure. The human mind and body are not made to endure pressure all the time, but the longer one lives on this earth, the more of this kind of trouble we face. It is good to know that God doesn't exclude the pressures of life from the realm of true suffering as Paul's experience amply demonstrates. We see it throughout the Acts and the epistles. Part of that was the intense pressure of ministering to the churches. Does it include the times when we face job pressure, tight finances, the stress of finding work when it is scarce, even the stresses parents face in raising a godly family in a world system that is against them from the start? Most definitely!

We tend to compartmentalize our lives into the spiritual and secular to make one kind of suffering not equal to the other. That is, we say that the sufferings of our daily grind don't really have anything to do with suffering for advancing the kingdom of God. But we aren't all preachers, teachers of the Bible, or evangelists. Our line of work involves *thlipsis* at times but is no less important in God's economy. In earning our living, we also are contributing to the support of others who may be directly involved in ministry. Since the great majority of us are not directly involved, I think God has a purpose for all of us in facing the pressures of life as part of advancing His kingdom.

Reading a little further in Paul's letter, we find that we carry the treasure of

> . . .*the knowledge of the glory of God in the face of*
> *Jesus Christ.* (2 Corinthians 4:6)

(that is, that God revealed Himself to us in Christ, the Son), but we carry that wonderful knowledge in these earthen vessels per Paul's metaphor. The word is used ordinarily for clay pots. In a household of that time, there might be containers made of silver or wood just for people to see and perhaps admire for their craftsmanship. But clay pots were just for a particular service, usually garbage or waste. They were breakable and not prominently displayed. And what comes with that life of service?

> *We are <u>hard-pressed</u> on every side . . .* (2 Corinthians 4:8)

It is *thlibo* in the Greek, a relative of *thlipsis* and has to do with a crowding that comes from wading through the troubles of life. Think of walking through a crowd of people at a big sporting event as you enter or exit the arena or when a theatre or night club is packed to capacity. In those examples, we feel perhaps a little uncomfortable with strangers so close by. When people are orderly, we are not crushed though you know it could easily happen if someone created a panic. Also, he writes, *"we are perplexed . . ."* We have the idea that the mind sometimes sees no way out of the crowd; we are at a loss mentally. We can't figure out why things go the way they do. Things just are not working out the way we had planned or hoped or even expected from God, and it perplexes our minds. It is a puzzle we can't solve.

Hardship

In 2 Corinthians 1:5 Paul introduces the *pathema* of Christ. Derived from *pathos*, we get our words empathy and sympathy from it. It can be thought of as something undergone, as in a hardship. It is also a term for suffering in general. God seems to be saying that even as He comforts us in the pressures we face (2 Corinthians 1:4), we also should comfort others in the hardships they face. Also, that the hardships we face are necessary if we are going to be able to help others in Christ. Just as the Father had to send the Son in the flesh to sympathize with our weakness (Hebrews 4:15), we cannot comfort those who suffer hardship unless we have at least been through it ourselves.

About the same time that Paul was writing to the Corinthians, he was also addressing the subject of *pathema* in his letter to the church in Rome. Here, he puts our hardships in this life in perspective:

> *For I consider that the sufferings* (pathema) *of this present time are not worthy to be compared with the glory which shall be revealed in us.* (Romans 8:18)

Have you considered whether the many hardships you face have actual eternal value?

The desert is meant to be a place of desolation and isolation. Part of that desolation can include the suffering of failing health, perhaps a kind of *pathema* because we are familiar with it in the context of pathology—the study of disease. A year after my wife's surgery, I was still unemployed and staring at the loss of medical insurance coverage while facing a deteriorating hernia. I scheduled surgery on my birthday. (What a great way to celebrate!) It was completed routinely and I recovered reasonably well. This was good since we were preparing for our son's wedding, now only two months away. Add to that, my wife was about to take on the responsibilities of managing a tutoring business full-time.

Shortly thereafter, I began to discover another health problem, a disease I hadn't the slightest idea existed until I began to research it on my own. Though it has been known by medical science for well over two hundred years, there is no cure for it. Turns out, it is not all that uncommon in men, especially as we age. But I would still be considered relatively young for this to happen at 55. My condition isn't life threatening like cancer, but it is certainly one of those problems that cause one to say, "Why me?" To this point, the answer lies only in the desert. And yes, I went to the physicians; they confirmed my diagnosis and offered what little they know as treatment. I made it a matter of prayer for healing, but the symptoms persisted. While I pursued healing, I also turned my thoughts once again to the purpose of this kind of suffering.

Perhaps a year later, we were returning from a visit with my mother-in-law, having learned that a very dear friend of hers was consumed by cancer. This, after having battled for years to near victory over it only to see things deteriorate rapidly. We could see she was heartbroken. The fragility and brevity of our lives are certainly among those things that God wants to show us in the desert days.

But until then, what do we do? The apostle Paul had an unnamed physical infirmity that stayed with him throughout his days of ministry, presumably to the end of his life (2 Corinthians 12:7). His example demonstrates the response we all should have.

> *Therefore I take pleasure in infirmities, in reproaches, in needs, in persecutions, in distresses for Christ's sake. For when I am weak, then I am strong.* (2 Corinthians 12:10)

We are to take pleasure in these things and not see them as judgments from God. Rather, they are the means by which His strength is shown. When we accept our weakness, we are no longer trying to fight God. We simply acquiesce to His will for the purpose of using us mightily. I think this is part of what JRR Tolkien was trying to say in the character of Bilbo Baggins in his novel, *The Hobbit*. Here was someone small, unskilled in battle who admitted his shortcomings and surrendered to the great adventure in life that God wants us to join in beating down the very gates of Hell (Tolkien was a Catholic academic who greatly influenced another academic, C.S. Lewis, in turning from atheism to Christ).

And what about the hardships involved in keeping a marriage going in the desert? When I lost my job in Idaho, my wife and I made the decision that she should fulfill her obligation to the tutoring business by staying in Idaho through the end of the school year since most of the clients were local school children and it was a growing business that year. Her days were long, sometimes not ending until 6 or 7 p.m. as she attended to the details of scheduling tutors, submitting invoices, rearranging scheduled times for clients, watching the budget, being janitor, and doing a little tutoring of children to fill in the gaps. I became the dinner cook, and she would come home famished, thankful for almost anything I prepared. (I am better at breakfast as my family will attest.) It was an awkward time for me, having been conditioned to the role of bread winner for decades, but we were thankful for God's provision.

Then God did an "out-of-the-blue" thing. Just as earlier in my career, I got a call from a headhunter that previously was unknown to me. I had not reached out to him, but a colleague of his on the other side of the country mentioned my name to him. I suppose I had supplied contact information several years earlier but had not spoken directly with him in over 15 years. Within a week, I was interviewing in Moses Lake, Washington. Several days later, I was boarding a flight back to home from an interview in Nevada, (let's be honest, nearly all of Nevada is desert), when I got a phone call with a generous offer from Moses Lake. Several days later, I got an offer from the Nevada company. I chose Moses Lake and started barely a month after I was apprised of the opening. My new job in Washington state began as the chill of winter was approaching and there were still seven months left in the school year. Because the one-way trip was 350 miles, I thought returning home every two weeks would work for my wife. The holidays would also give us a little more time together before the end of the year, but this was uncharted territory for our marriage as we looked at the math . . . a mere four days out of every month spent together. By the time

Christmas rolled around, my wife was feeling the strain of our separation, so I committed to making the trip home every weekend.

After the new year began and for the next 20 weeks, I would leave work on Friday a half hour before dark, (in my beloved Buick Century, then approaching 225,000 miles on the odometer), arrive at midnight and leave late Sunday afternoon—driving mostly in the dark and arriving at my rented, converted garage apartment in Moses Lake at bedtime. I logged over 17,000 miles in that time. It was truly a unique period in my life, one I would not trade away easily because it was such hard work.

But I did it out of the need to keep our marriage healthy. The demands of my wife's job kept her from taking the best care of herself so I also delighted in bringing home groceries she didn't have time or energy to shop for but would keep her going—things she enjoyed like soup and yogurt bought at bargain prices from my favorite little store in Moses Lake. I would stock the pantry with what seemed ridiculous amounts of cereal (but in time proved to be just enough). It wasn't all we did—weekend visits and communication on poor quality cell phone calls isn't sufficient. The Bible commands husbands to dwell with their wives according to knowledge; that is, getting to know them, their needs, desires, hopes and fears. After 30 years of marriage, I knew a few things about this woman and one of those was her emotional makeup. I never satisfied her emotional needs perfectly, but it's incumbent on husbands to do their best at it. During this time, I was thankful that our daughter lived close by and visited during the week because living alone can be frightening at times. You certainly don't sleep well apart from your mate.

It took a month to shop around and finally get connected to internet service and find the right webcam, but the second most important thing we did was visit each night via Skype. As technology goes, it wasn't perfect, but it's free and a marvelous invention! Without regular communication, a marriage doesn't stand a chance because it meets a complex emotional need. Talking about our day was good but seeing my wife's face and the sadness or happiness in her expressions was an important connection. We also prayed together this way. I also made it a habit to call most mornings and send her off to her day. It was necessary to encourage each other. Try or even imagine neglecting talking to your spouse for a week and see what becomes of your marriage. It might continue to exist, but it won't be strong. The point I am making is that separation of the sort that is forced upon your marriage (in our case, by the economy) will make you understand what it means to work at a marriage. The saying, "Absence makes the heart grow fonder," is quaint, but I think applies more to the courting couple. Absence in a marriage makes for a lot of hard work.

Traveling so much on the same lonely roads back and forth had its risks and rewards. Nearly all of it was on freeway, traveling over the desertscape of eastern Washington and Oregon. The Blue Mountains in fall and spring are a beautiful part of the drive, but they can be treacherous in the wintertime, especially at night. On at least three occasions, I drove back to Moses Lake in winter storms that manifested themselves on that range. My night vision was not as good as it used to be. Add any kind of snowfall and the glare was blinding to me. My family and I had driven through bad snowstorms in Wyoming before, but now I was faced with that possibility almost every weekend that winter. The stretch from LaGrande to Pendleton was white knuckle on these occasions as the plow crews had not hit the roads yet. One trip I will never forget offered me the challenge of driving this section through about six inches of fresh snow and accumulating rapidly. The only way you stay on the road is by seeing the reflector posts which don't come nearly as often as you want them to in those conditions.

After 30 miles of this, you arrive at Cabbage Hill, a well-known switchback grade on I-84 heading into Pendleton. Here, you might encounter a variety of conditions. On this particular trip, I thought it fortunate to be following a pickup's taillights down the grade in near zero visibility when we both found ourselves off the road and into a runaway truck ramp. Fortunately, we were able to back out and make it down the hill only to find the road west of town to be covered with frozen slush. And just when I thought that I was out of the worst of it, the last part of highway to Moses Lake offered me a freak storm that was blowing through a stretch of only ten miles, but it seemed like 100. As I approached the top of one hill (again, unplowed), a flatbed truck had jackknifed across the road, blocking all traffic and forcing me to drive in the borrow ditch next to a farmer's field for about a half mile. On another occasion, I encountered the infamous Cabbage Hill fog that was freezing to the road surface. As I crept down the hill, I could feel the car slip and slide, knowing that I had semis behind me that would not see me until they were nigh on my bumper. The thought of meeting my end plunging off the road and down the embankment was certainly there.

These were the times that made me want to give up on the Moses Lake venture, especially not really understanding yet why God wanted me there. But it was hardship with a purpose, as are all hardships in God's economy.

> *Yet in all these things we are more than conquerors through Him who loved us.* (Romans 8:37)

I am not exaggerating the difficult stretch this was for us. At the same time, these trips gave me hours (usually the first hour or two of every trip) in intimate prayer with God sometimes to pour out my complaint, sometimes to try coming closer to understanding His purposes in suffering. But they were times of prayer such as I had not had in many years nor have I had since because I could pour out my heart to Him (Psalm 62:8) and spend miles on the road in supplication for others.

After seven long months of this, my wife was finally able to join me in Moses Lake. In God's providence, the source of income from her Nampa employment was soon to dry up. She was coming to Moses Lake, regardless, but it meant another year of renting and moving all our earthly possessions to a house in one of the oldest parts of town. To her, it meant the hardship of unpacking our stuff while leaving much of it in boxes just to live in someone else's house for at least another year. We made the difficult decision to keep our Nampa house off the market for a year. From the housing bust that began in 2007, Canyon County had seen one of the worst declines in real estate value nationwide. At one point, the value of our home in Nampa had declined nearly 45%. Of course, we weren't alone in that. Eventually, our little subdivision of perhaps 40 homes had up to eight for sale at the same time, many of them in foreclosure, some on short sale. We talked with realtors at intervals, trying to watch the market for an opportunity to sell, only to find that the neighbor's HUD foreclosure meant our house could fetch no better price for the next three months.

Meanwhile, we learned to enjoy the simple pleasures of our Moses Lake rental which included the city park only two blocks away where we listened to concerts in the summer. The house also had peach and pear trees that produced a bumper crop which we canned and gave away to our heart's content. I also had a small garden patch where I planted sweet corn for the first time in many years and not to happen again for many years. One year later, we were consumed with the upheaval of buying and moving to another house while selling our home in Nampa and moving our daughter to a new apartment. It was physically, mentally, and emotionally arduous. At the end of July, we were exhausted. No one thinks they are going to be moving and starting new lives as they approach 60 years of age, but I found a few people in the intervening years in our same age bracket that had done the very same thing. Such are the economic hard times that God uses to disperse His people for His plans and purposes.

I have spent a lot of time here on *pathema* suffering, not to bore the reader with these accounts, but to make a broader point about trials. Do we see the grace of God in them? Along the way, I wrote down something I remembered Charles Swindoll had said. "God not only plans the length of a test, but the depth."

Study for the Exam

Trials are further spoken of in the New Testament by degree, I think. *Dokime* (2 Corinthians 8:2) or *dokimion* (1 Peter 1:7) refer to 'a putting to the test' and originally have to do with examination before a board of review for an advanced degree. It is a test for trustworthiness or an experiment for proof. But it is not as if God were capriciously experimenting on us. Rather, He is doing it so we know that we can bear the load and stand the pressure. It isn't for His knowledge. God already knows all things. Rather, it is so we come to the point of confidence through added knowledge and experience that we are ready to do battle. It is important that we have this confidence when facing life's battles, especially in spiritual warfare where it is easy to get discouraged. Matthew Henry wrote,

> "The faith of good people is tried that they themselves may have the comfort of it, God the Glory of it, and others the benefit of it." (Matthew Henry's Commentary on the Whole Bible, Hendrickson Publishers Inc., Copyright 1991, 10th printing, pg. 2423)

Without these kinds of tests, God cannot use us to pass along the faith to the next generation. There must be proof that we know the cost of our faith in Christ so others after us can see its value.

When I took the job in Moses Lake, I had been out of the work force for a long time. You might say I had lost a few steps in the year and a half following the Great Recession. My new situation was project manager at a silicon refinery. The learning curve was steep. There were rigorous-process safety protocols for every project, a complex production process to learn, new business management software, and team forming with people I did not know. I had only been on the job for three months when the engineering manager asked me to take on a support role for projects in research and development. It meant moving my office to the R&D facility and not having immediate access to my colleagues for technical support for a year.

I was now out of the frying pan and into the fire, learning about clean-room design and complicated specifications for materials with which I had little familiarity. I also had to find vendors for custom-designed equipment. There were days I would start in the dark of morning and leave after dark in the evening completely overwhelmed with everything and crying out to God for wisdom. It was a *dokime* test for the next year to prepare me for the rigors of this season of life. It was a challenging time, yet wonderful to see how God answered my need by giving keen insight and the ability to generate useful ideas for my employer.

Trapped and You Can't Get Out

An interesting but little used word for suffering as anguish is *stenochoria*. Once in Romans 8:35 and again in 2 Corinthians 6:4, it refers to being in a narrow place. Think of it as a place where there is no way out. Militarily, it is depicted by a narrow canyon where an army is trapped because they have no room to maneuver. In the untamed west, ranchers would corral their livestock in box canyons. The passage in these geological features becomes narrower the farther in you travel. There were a few of these canyons near where we lived in Green River, Wyoming. Some are used today for horse corrals.

Here is the sense that we are trapped, and there is no way out. Three of the five times it is used, it appears with *thlipsis*, suggesting that it follows from the outward pressures of life leading to internal anguish of the spirit or mind. I read in the newsletters of the Voice of the Martyrs about the persecution of saints in our day in foreign

A Box Canyon

lands where some spend years in prison for proclaiming the Christian faith. Their stories include the honest confession of having to deal with depression upon their release because of the way they were treated and because they were separated from family for so long. This is *stenochoria,* and we must not think that it is wrong to be in this place. Paul was there as stated in 2 Corinthians 6:4. Christians experience depression because they are human. I think we can all agree that it is wrong to stay there, hence the need to seek help and healing. But it is a real experience. Webster's dictionary defines anguish as "extreme pain, distress or anxiety."

The word picture is clearer with a breakdown of its two Greek components. *Stenos* we use in our word 'stenography,' that is, writing in shorthand. Of course, this is a concept foreign to our day of computers and word processing but two generations ago it was a useful skill all over the business world. My wife even took a year of shorthand in high school (and taught me how to write 'I love you' which I used in notes to her). My dad was accomplished in shorthand because he wanted to use it in college note taking. He continued to use it well into his later years. *Chora* is the area between two lines, like a steno pad where we see narrow spaces in which to do our writing. To postulate a little further, *choreia* is used in our word choreography, meaning to plan out a series of dance steps to tell a story. This brings to mind the amazing work of artists like Gene Kelly in the film *Singin' In The Rain.* But the point is that, in life, we are sometimes moving through narrow passageways where we feel there is no escape. We don't know what is ahead, try to figure a way out, but can't come up with the solution. From this, we get our expression of "feeling boxed-in." It is an internal trial brought on by the pressures of life, but we must trust that God is planning every step.

For our six years in Moses Lake, we experienced this constriction. Though I saw the struggles of my employer's business as the years ensued, I came to understand that it was the Lord's leading to go there, work in a new industry, and bring my wife. Part of that realization didn't dawn on me until my wife volunteered at a local Christian school, tutored some of the children, and then became a full-time teacher which she hadn't done since the early years of our marriage. I could see God's hand in all of that, how Jesus had a need and wanted us to be a part of meeting that need. Even in the most perplexing of times, it fills your heart to know that. Even when employment comes and goes, there is great peace in knowing you carried out the work that He called you to do.

And it was looking like this could be a good way to finish our careers. We were in the peak earning years that most couples anticipate. I still had a good mind and a good work ethic. Professionally speaking, I had bushels of experience and judgment that were finally clicking. I was coming up with solutions, in fact, moving rather confidently into the role of problem solver— making sound choices on projects while working efficiently in my role. Then the clouds continued to gather over the silicon manufacturing business until my professional bubble popped again. In the grand scheme of things, it didn't matter. To most people we knew, it didn't seem to matter at all. But I felt isolated 'between the lines' once again. This time, I was about to learn things heretofore undiscovered about the desert. I was laid off from a project manager position in the engineering department at the age of 60. It seemed God's plan was to subject me to the ignominy of discovering that no one is interested in hiring older people, even in an economy that most considered good (with unemployment said to be near historic lows). The walls of life were narrowing in on me, constricting my options.

After seven months of slogging through the job market, there were a few phone interviews and a couple of tentative offers that were quietly pulled back. I found recruiters would not stay on my case for long . . . without any explanation. Business contacts would return one phone call and perhaps reply to one email. After that, silence. When I finally found someone willing to take a chance on me, it came from a cold call I made back in Idaho and there was no formal position for which to apply. I was hired, but into a non-engineering position. My wife was hired to teach at a struggling private school after we moved, but it folded at the end of her first year there. For sure, God was showing me this part of the desert for a reason. First, I am not the only one to experience this, and it helps me relate to others—age discrimination is common, but difficult to prove in a court. Second, it turns out that this was an intense spiritual battle. I engaged the prayer support of a half dozen men I knew from past to present. I know some of them continued fervently in that because they would occasionally ask me how the search was going. I was drained of energy many times and often asked our heavenly Father for new direction in life, realizing that it was not necessary for me to pursue career as if it were an idol. Still, I worried that my life's work was coming to an end, without fanfare or recognition from anyone.

The employment I got from the cold call didn't even last that long as I saw the small engineering firm double in size over the next year and a half only to find that the growth was mismanaged. Staff had to be reduced by 30%, and pay cuts were implemented across the board. The economy at large was still in good shape, and we had just enjoyed a wonderful catered Christmas party together. It was a humbling time for the company president. I volunteered reduced hours for the sake of the younger men with families, but he let me go with my notice coming by email.

Not only was it confirmation of the continuing desert in life, but it came several years before one "normally" retires in America. My wife and I were unemployed now and scrambling to find adequate medical insurance. God was shaking the tree once again. What I see more clearly now is that God doesn't promise all of His children a storybook career until the day we officially retire with the gold watch and a banquet in our honor (culmination of the so-called "American dream"). Instead, He promises to meet our needs. I admit to some envy for those I know whose careers had no setbacks, but I am also reminded of Jesus' words to Peter when he questioned what would become of John (John 21:21)—in essence, "What is that to you? You follow Me." In God's providence and sovereignty, the paths of each one in His family will most likely not be the same.

Now that I have painted the picture of two sixty-two-year-old people without work, here is the lesson: God was taking us through a trial of being boxed in, not knowing how to get out despite our efforts to find that passage. He was pushing us to further understand what it means to walk by faith and not by sight even though we thought that lesson had been covered long ago. Still, it is a light affliction compared to what others suffer. I wrote this at a time when our Christian brothers and sisters in the Middle East were being run out of their communities by barbarians and had no way to make a living, for years just surviving in refugee camps.

Loss as Suffering

Philippians chapter 3 has always been valuable to me, but its truth in the desert became more intimate through the pain of suffering loss. Paul begins talking about his Jewish pedigree and all he had gained as a respected Pharisee, member of the tribe of Benjamin and so forth. Then he says:

> *But what things were gain to me, these I have counted loss for Christ. Yet indeed I also count all things loss for the excellence of the knowledge of Christ Jesus my Lord for whom I have suffered the loss of all things . . .* (Philippians. 3:7, 8)

Let's stop there for now and look at the word "loss." (Sorry, academics first.) In the first two uses, we have the Greek word *zemia* preceeded by *hegeomai*. We use the term 'hegemony' and Webster's dictionary defines it as influence or control over a country or another group of people. Paul, a Roman citizen, understood the militaristic Roman rule of the day and used military terms often in his letters. Here, he conveys the idea of commanding the loss in a violent manner. In a sense, it is taken from him by another kingdom. After all, the account of his conversion on the road to Damascus was dramatic and sudden. In the eyes of our Savior, there was no other way to do it. That might help in understanding Jesus when He said,

> *And from the days of John the Baptist until now the kingdom of heaven <u>suffers violence, and the violent take it by force</u>.* (Matthew 11:12, emphasis mine)

My view is that the underlined phrases can be interpreted to mean the kingdom of God is 'pressed into and the energetic get all caught up in it.' It must become all that matters to us if it is to have any impact on our world. Certainly, Paul could also be saying that he had to willfully, and with some internal struggle, leave all his former life behind.

The third use of "loss" in Philippians 3:7 and 8 is the next word after *zemia* in the concordance and therefore related—*zemioo*. Injury is the primary meaning, but it also has the element of being cast away. It is a form of suffering in that we have to willfully cast off all that we hold dear before we can gain "the excellence of the knowledge of Christ Jesus our Lord. That which seems so harsh about Jesus' words in Matthew 10:37 (loving family more than Jesus) is corroborated by Paul in this passage. For starters, his conversion to following Christ meant the loss of prestige. This is why he says, "concerning the law, a Pharisee." Pharisees came from the scribes in contrast to Sadducees who came from the priestly line. Scribes and Pharisees were the religious lawyers. They knew the Jewish rabbinic law (Talmud) backward and forward. It was a respected position that Paul immediately left behind. Furthermore, scholars have suggested that to hold that office, a man had to be married. We don't know what happened to Paul's marriage, but it is possible he had to give that up as well if his wife did not follow him into the faith.

I used to assume that this was a matter of fact with Paul—that he made this transition without trouble. I now see in the reading of it here in Philippians that it was gut-wrenching change in his life. True, we are told in Acts that he immediately began preaching the Gospel in Damascus. I can't help but believe that his time in the Arabian Desert followed this. Perhaps part of that experience was dealing with the losses. Think about it for a minute. What was this time for him if not to learn to slay those things of the past while getting to know Christ, the one he met on the road to Damascus? Yes, to know Him and the power of His resurrection! It seems entirely likely that this desert sojourn was God's time with him to make known all the mysteries of Christ. And so it should be for us a time to grasp all those things we had taken for granted about our God and His salvation.

Loss is real for us as people. When you build up so much that you treasured in life and then see some of it or all of it leave, there is loss with which to deal. Our emotional make-up requires it. I don't think God is saying that we are expected to just walk away from loss without emotion. Sometimes, it is that easy. Most of the time, it is not. So how do you get through it?

First, we need to pray and enlist the prayer of others when we feel the sting of broken dreams or unwelcome change in our lives. And that prayer isn't so much, "Lord, help me through this" as it is, "Lord, make Your strength perfect in my weakness."

Second, accept grieving the loss as a natural part of the process. Norman Wright wrote:

> "Tears are the vehicles God has equipped us with to express the deepest feelings where words cannot." (*Recovering from Losses in Life*, H. Norman Wright, copyright 1991, republished 2006, Fleming H. Revell Co.)

We were also surprised at the role grieving plays and how necessary it is during times of loss. As we closed and taped the last boxes from our moves both out of Wyoming to Idaho, then later from Idaho to Washington, my wife and I sat down. It was only after all that physically exhausting effort that we both released a torrent of tears, literally weeping until we were emotionally drained as well. Yes, even me, the strong man of the family. There was no one else in the room except Jesus. It was unexpected at both times, just flowing as we prayed out our grief and thanksgiving, though we still didn't quite understand what lay ahead.

It can even be those times when you are burying the pet that has been killed by a hit-and-run driver. In all these kinds of situations, we probably feel a little guilty being upset by what others would say is trivial. It isn't as if it is real loss. You might say this is a kind of emotional suffering, the situation where feelings are finally catching up with facts. For the benefit of the men here, let me add this: don't be afraid to cry. Be especially vulnerable with your wife. It won't lessen her view of you. She will see that her man has a tender heart and needs her strength to stand and face the deserts of this life. In these times, let the tears flow without shame.

We eventually understand that the reason we put losses behind us is because it is the way to knowing the power of Christ's resurrection and the fellowship of His sufferings (Philippians 3:8-10). The Greek word for "know" in this passage is *gnosko* and doesn't stop at head knowledge; rather, it is intimate understanding. When our identity is tied to what we do or who we know or how much we have or even our self-esteem, a loss of any of those things can be destabilizing or at least perplexing. I have struggled with this through the many employment changes I experienced.

Accumulating losses can have the effect of killing your momentum in life. God has had to bring me to the point of not being stuck on what other people may think about me but that my value comes from Him alone. The problem comes when we get caught on the world system of valuing that which is temporary. In America for sure, it is particularly easy for men to define themselves by what they do for work. It has been engrained in our national psyche but is no less a lie from the world system, if not borderline idolatry. Still, to get to the place of leaving our losses in the dung heap of history, we may need help, especially when the loss is traumatic.

A Purifying Fire

I have not said much about trial by fire because I probably have not experienced that in a very real sense yet. *Purosis* is the word (used only in 1 Peter 4:12) and I believe should be reserved for suffering that derives from persecution for our faith in Christ. This whole letter from Peter is written to the dispersed church at the time—dispersed because of great persecution. This kind of trial results in purifying pictured as the refinement of gold to remove contaminating metals to make it more valuable. The silicon business previously mentioned used a chemical process at high temperatures to reduce metal contaminants, not only to increase its market value, but to make it more useful as a raw material in semi-conductor manufacturing. It was a multi-step process—a good metaphor for purging from our lives as Christians that which hinders our usefulness in advancing the kingdom.

And what's more, Peter gets us back to this realization that we are not to be surprised when it happens. As previously mentioned, we are prone to think of suffering in this manner as counter to God's will. But Peter points out that suffering resulting from our association with Christ, is nothing of which to be ashamed (1 Peter 4:16). It's a refining fire even in America where our increasingly hedonistic culture grows more intolerant of Christians speaking out for God's standard of righteousness just as much as it is for the Church in countries under the oppressive thumb of Islam or communism.

The context here is, in fact, being *"reproached for the name of Christ,"* (1 Peter 4:14). Does it mean that we have not suffered a purifying of our faith unless we are reviled personally? I don't believe so. Because

> . . . *if one member suffers, all the members suffer*
> *with it.* (1 Corinthians 12:26)

We feel the reproach of our suffering brethren. Perhaps it is a brother held in a Turkish prison and tortured there for his conviction that Christ is Lord, not Allah. It might be the reproach we experience when our culture embraces homosexuality as an acceptable lifestyle in direct rebellion with God's Word. When the drift of our society is in this direction, you know you are on the brink of suffering in the refining fire that is *purosis*.

Related to this kind of persecution suffering is *dioko* and refers figuratively to being pursued as in a hunt. In other places, it speaks to the Christian's need to follow or "press hard after" as in

> . . . *press toward the goal for the prize of the upward*
> *call of God in Christ Jesus.* (Philippians 3:14)

In most of the third world today, those who live for and worship Jesus are targeted for killing, maiming, forced exile, or discrimination to the extent that they lose their jobs or are forced to live in squalor. Examples include the Coptic Christians of modern Egypt or the people of Sudan forced into the Nuba Mountains and, even there, have been pursued in bombing runs and attacks by the armies of the Islamic ruling powers in Khartoum. In the so-called 'developed' countries of the world, including the United States, the forces of atheism and secularism put people in power who wage a war against people of faith with the goal of removing them from influence in public life. In one, physical force is used. In the other, lawyers and politicians. Make no mistake, in both cases, it is *dioko*.

A final note on this word study - Appendix I contains a comprehensive list of New Testament references about suffering.

Sufferings in Perspective

In this chapter, we have learned that many kinds of suffering impinge on our lives. Each is an aspect of hardship. But where is God in all this? I was drawn to reflect on a tremendous portion of Scripture as I was pining in the desert wondering if my physical existence really mattered anymore (call it what you will, depression, etc.; these are the things you think as you are being dragged through the desert).

In 2 Corinthians chapter 4, Paul has us take stock in the promise that our sufferings are light afflictions, working (*katergadzomai*) for us an eternal weight (*baros*) of glory (4:17). Why did Paul choose these words? We get our English words 'ergonomics' (working with the hands) and 'bar' (a unit of measure for pressure) from these. I like to think that God is reaching down, touching us when we endure hardships of pathema and adding to our understanding the glory we will see in heaven. It helps us look forward with hope, but also to look at the unseen things after this life (4:18). That word comes from *skopeo* from which we get our English, "scope." When looking down the road or planning a trip, we 'scope it out,' don't we? The heaven-bound person is focused on what lies ahead in God's place of eternal glory even as we endure the sufferings and hardships of the world we see with our eyes.

It's another one of those lessons that you have heard many times, but it doesn't get hammered home until you are in the middle of a crisis and it grabs your attention. We must realize that our existence here is temporary and cannot outlast the storms that rip and tear our bodies, no matter the advances of medical science. It's a perspective that's important to our journey.

Continuing, Paul writes:

> *For we know that if our earthly house, this tent* (skenos, from which we get our word "skin"), *is destroyed, we have a building from God, a house not made with hands, eternal in the heavens.* (2 Corinthians 5:1, parentheses mine)

I love the analogy here. Of course, we know that Paul earned at least a portion of his livelihood through the trade of tent-making (Acts 18:3). I have owned several tents and have always been a tent camper. As I get older, the thought of trailer camping appeals more and more to me. But it is an awesome experience to be in your tent in the middle of the wilderness at night during a thunderstorm. The wind and rain beat against it, but you take some comfort in the meager shelter it provides, knowing that the storm will pass. It isn't the most comfortable of quarters, but it goes where wheels do not go. In Paul's day, tents were probably a more common form of living quarters, especially for the poor. For forty years in the wilderness, we know this is how the Israelites lived. No permanent dwellings there. Even God went with them in a tent!

Tents come in many varieties of design. I wonder sometimes what designs Paul made and sold. He made these with his hands—

no sewing machines then. As an itinerant missionary for much of his ministry, Paul traveled over the mountains of Asia Minor and Greece and knew the experience of 'camping.' No doubt he saw the destruction and deterioration of tents many times. The context here is that our bodies are just tents. They are temporary dwellings. At some point, through use and exposure, they begin to flap in the wind and become tattered. Sometimes, a storm will take them in an instant, before their usefulness is over. The point is that, eventually, our fleshly dwelling is destroyed but then we get a house made by Jesus, the master carpenter, creator, and designer! Why wouldn't we groan and pine for that (2 Corinthians 5:2)? As previously mentioned, I once rented a house, all the while owning a house hundreds of miles away. The circumstances of life prevented me from living in that house, but I still longed for it.

Next, Paul adds this curious phrase:

> . . .*if indeed having been clothed, we shall not be found naked. For we who are in this tent groan, being burdened, not because we want to be unclothed, but further clothed, that mortality may be swallowed up by life.* (2 Corinthians 5:3-4)

Some interpret the nakedness referred to here as a disembodied state after physical death in which the believer, prior to the return of Christ, is still without an eternal body and therefore exists only as spirit before God. You could also say that we have an instinct to hide our physical nakedness. In modesty, we don't want people to see it. In the same way, we don't want our faults and weaknesses to be evident to others. After so much time and effort keeping up appearances and maintaining our body, don't we get tired of it and just look forward to the day when we slip out of this earthly body and into one that no longer needs so much attention? It's not that we just want to hang it up. While here on Earth, death is not a threshold we are eager to cross. We have family that need us, perhaps things we would still like to accomplish. But we get weary of the fight at times and feel like giving up, even to the point of longing for the eternal body that is guaranteed to last forever.

It is our desire to leave these bodies and have the better, eternal body that God provides. In this, the Bible gives perspective on how our culture overvalues the physical existence and exhibits such vanity in everything from appearance to possessions that we use to define ourselves. Instead, as Paul concludes, we should be

> . . .*well pleased, rather, to be absent from the body and to be present with the Lord.* (2 Corinthians 5:8)

In a desert time, when you realize all you had built before is slipping away or that you may have to leave it behind, you take hold of His words and say, "This is truth . . . the other is not."

Some Final Thoughts

Here in the discussion of suffering is a good place to reflect and say no one in the midst of suffering thinks of it academically. We want answers and many times, they don't come. My wife and I certainly didn't ask for suffering in our lives. Nobody does, but almost everyone experiences it to one degree or another. As mentioned, the New Testament scriptures often refer to suffering as something to be endured, albeit with joy. To the latter point, I think Joni Tada says it well as she was experiencing a period in her life of intense physical pain:

> "God uses suffering to sandblast you and me. There is nothing like real hardship to strip off the veneer in which you and I so carefully cloak ourselves. Heartache and physical pain reach below the superficial surface places of our lives, stripping away years of accumulated indifference and neglect. When pain and problems press us up against a holy

God, suffering can't help but strip away years of dirt. Affliction has a way of jackhammering our character, shaking us up and loosening our grip on everything we hold tightly. Where's the benefit? The process of divine sandblasting can reveal something quite beautiful - not only on the outside but on the inside. And people may find themselves seeing something in you – some grace or quality of life – they had never seen before, or hadn't seen for years and years."

"There's something sweet and precious about cracking open your heart and giving your affection to the Savior in the midst of a difficult or painful situation that takes a simple testimony like yours and pushes it over the top. Because there's nothing like a song of praise rising out of brokenness that brings glory to our God." (Excerpted from *A Place of Healing*, pp. 54, 129, © 2010 Joni Eareckson Tada. Used by permission of David C. Cook. May not be further reproduced. All rights reserved)

When you see others not going through the same kind of trials that you are experiencing, the flesh tries to assert itself. The natural thing is to ponder like King David when he saw that and asked, "Why do the wicked prosper?" Our first inclination is to blame others rather than look inward. Fairness is not an attribute of our God. Justice, yes . . . fairness, no. The two are not the same. In our generations of late, there is a preoccupation with fairness to the extent that society is being driven to demand equality of outcomes and not just equality of opportunity. This is being perverted into so-called "social justice" as if that is what will bring true happiness. Real justice is defined as wrong punished without prejudice. Unfortunately, our sinful nature too often interprets this as fairness. We all want fairness but are disappointed to learn time and again that the adage, "Life is not fair" doesn't satisfy us or answer our questions.

Still, I sometimes think God may be visiting the sins of my youth on me or, worse yet on my children similar to the proverb:

> *The fathers have eaten sour grapes, and the children's teeth are set on edge.* (Jeremiah. 31:29)

This is a biblical truth, but it can lead to a wrong understanding of God. It is not wrong to do an examination of our lives before God. It can fulfill the purpose of getting us to recognize sin, bring repentance and then restoration. The enemy loves to use this angle of attack; that is, God judging our sins. Always framing it this way is wrong because it often leads to seeing God as a curmudgeon. However, to discern the difference between it and other causes of suffering is often easier said than done. After all, we see David, himself, silent toward God because he thought God was judging him for his sin at one point in his life (Psalm 39:7-13). And what can we say if that is the case? David felt this way about it:

> *You make his beauty melt away like a moth.* (Psalm 39:11)

What an apt description of our desert selves. As in ancient times, so it is now that a moth illustrates a short-lived existence—our youthful appearance and vigor quickly gone.

Near Christmas 2012, a good friend of mine from high school lost a son to a tragic automobile accident when he was just entering young manhood. It gives the heart great pause. My sister-in-law died from a blood cancer before she was fifty; she was dedicated to Jesus, but didn't live to see any of her eventual 15 grandchildren. In the light of that, isn't everything we do to survive or make significance of ourselves just a little vain? God graciously allowed me to see my dad one more time in his last days after experiencing a severe stroke. He was nearly 94 and had a long and rewarding life, but his appearance was a stark reminder of how our body can so quickly fade away when God says our time is over. Confronting the reality of your parents' dying days is also one of those things that, in the middle of everything else desert, show losses that seem to be just piling up.

As I was completing the second draft on this book, a global pandemic of the COVID-19 virus was ensuing beginning in January of 2020. This was one of those historic events that you never think you would see in your lifetime. Our nation's state and local governments were implementing non-voluntary isolation orders. 'Social distancing' became more than a buzzword. It was surreal. Churches were not holding services. Nearly all schools were shut down for the remainder of the academic year. Graduations and major sporting events were cancelled, including the NCAA's basketball championships. By the tens of thousands, people were being tested for the virus. The news business was totally preoccupied with it for the remainder of the year. Shelves for essential dry goods like sugar, flour, and toilet paper at grocery stores were bare for weeks from shoppers hoarding in panic. Non-essential businesses were shut down—all in the effort to snuff out the spread of the virus. Many kinds of suffering were happening. People felt the *stenochoria* of being trapped in their homes. There was real *pascho* and *pathema* in the sickness and death from it, though comparisons with other pandemics would eventually show that it was not the worst. Because of government mandated restrictions, most dine-in restaurants were closed, and businesses were lost along with livelihoods. There was the resulting *thlipsis* of worrying about paying bills and putting food on the table, even in my own family.

It is interesting to note that God is to be blessed not because He <u>delivers</u> us from our trials, but because He <u>comforts</u> us in them (2 Corinthians 1:3). Have you ever thought of trials in your life as one of the mighty works of God? Psalm 66 illustrates this beautifully. It is about praising God for His awesome works . . . and among those listed are trial and affliction (vs 11, 12), leading us through it and bringing us to a place of *"rich fulfillment."* He declares the act of what God did for his soul (vs. 16), how he cried out to God and how He was praised (vs. 17), and finally how God attended to his prayer (vs. 19).

Even with more biblical knowledge about trials, we are still human and therefore persist in asking the question, "Why?" Or, "Why me?" In thinking about part of the reason for our trials, we can't underestimate the value of our response to God's kingdom. Perhaps there are those in my own family who look on (even from afar) still wondering if faith in our God is worth it. Maybe they have reasoned Him out but are still looking for a reason to believe. When they see a response of joy or at least continued belief on our part when bad things happen, they have three choices:

- Continued ambivalence
- Deepened cynicism ("How can I believe in a God who would do that?")
- Say, "I want to surrender to that God if He gives such peace."

When people try to argue against the existence of God because (they reason) a good God would not allow suffering, we understand that His goodness has nothing to do with it. In a fallen world, suffering is exactly what you would expect to see.

CHAPTER 4

FAITH, HOPE AND HAPPINESS

The longer our desert tour persists, the more we struggle with the things we need most—faith and hope. And we all struggle with the loss of happiness. When this condition persists, we long to see the horizon where our mind and spirit will be refreshed again. It serves us well to understand the role each of these has in our lives.

Faith

Looking at when the children of Israel were brought into the Wilderness of Sinai, sometimes we are tempted to think it was for their lack of faith in Yahweh and for their sinful rebellion. Certainly, their stay in the desert was prolonged because of those things, but God's original intention was to use the wilderness experience to draw them to Himself and show them they must be totally dependent on Him. It was intended to prepare them for real worship and godly living in the Promised Land. In short, they were not ready when they left Egypt. They would have quickly fallen prey to the pagan rites and lifestyles of the region. They didn't have the spiritual muscle to resist. Sadly, a whole generation was lost because they didn't realize that through the desert experience, God was with them both in person (think cloud by day and pillar of fire by night) and in purpose. He didn't just say, "Go into the desert, and I will see you on the other side."

It seems that the faith of those wanderers in Sinai (and ours) was grounded in the things of this life. The hardships were to them a sign that God wasn't with them because they could not see God wanting to separate them from earthly comfort and desires of the flesh; that is, to discipline them for their good. I think it is the reason they resorted to paganism in creating the golden calf for worship, something they could see, touch, and bow down to. Similarly, Paul writes to the Philippians that our adversaries (think, the world system) see our predicaments as judgments when we show fear in the midst of them rather than acknowledging and looking for the salvation of God in them. See Philippians 1:28, 29.

As I contemplated the journey of Israel out of Egypt and listened to others who visited the sites there, I wondered why a journey that should only take perhaps a week (on foot from Egypt to the Promised Land) was turned into one that consumed forty years. Even the long way around was only intended by God to take perhaps a year—enduring the rigors of the vast Sinai wilderness. In His mercy, God took the edge off so many times by miraculously providing what they needed and sometimes giving in to their wants if only to teach them that too much of a good thing is not good (e.g., the quail feast—see Exodus 16 for that story). I think at times they got worried that the desert was going to consume them, hence their complaining about the hardship they were enduring.

In pictures, Mount Sinai is not one mountain, but literally a range that is high and parched, stretching out for miles. I have been to some high and isolated places in the Bridger and Selway Wilderness areas of Wyoming and Idaho, but there are pristine lakes that you can fish, and it isn't too far to get back to civilization if you have to. Even today, Sinai is not like that. Perhaps a few Bedouins now and again who make their living as goat herders, but it is a hostile place. For sure, it was a place to learn to lean on God or die.

Even the lessons God had for them were not intended to take 40 years. At some point, a wilderness journey becomes too long for a reason and that reason usually has something to do with unbelief in what God is doing. We want to shy away from that possibility, but there is no mistaking that God deals with His people that way at times. Still, I think because of some misapplied Calvinism in our theology, we take it too far. We start believing that a struggle in life means God is punishing us. It is our Gentile way of thinking that leads to viewing struggle wrongly.

When we read the Gospels, it helps to view things from a first-century cultural perspective because that is the stage for their writing—in particular, their Jewish culture. The parables of Jesus are all framed this way because the common people could immediately relate by way of everyday life experiences that Jesus used to communicate truth about God. We don't use the word much outside of Bible studies, but it is helpful to parse the original Greek. *Paraballos* has the familiar prefix *para* (coming alongside). B*allos* means to throw. What do you do with a ball? So, we are throwing alongside—comparing one thing to another more common, everyday thing. It might be apples to apples. It might be apples to oranges, but it creates a hook for our memory.

Luke 18 begins with a lesson Jesus is teaching His disciples about persisting in prayer with God. This is one of those parables that we scratch our heads at because Jesus appears to be showing God as an unjust judge. It makes us uncomfortable because we can't explain how God might be framed that way. The story implies that the judge is literally corrupt, perhaps to the extent that he is even taking bribes. After all, down through the ages, money has bought influence with the authorities. In this case, he is dealing with a widow who has no power because her status came from her husband (still the case in many countries, which shows how timeless the Word of God is for application). All she had was a loud voice and persistence. She had been thrust into a situation over which she had no control. She was forced into her own desert of widowhood without choice.

In her case, imagine for a moment that the adversary mentioned was someone taking advantage of her financially, perhaps depriving her of the means to support herself. Whatever the circumstances, Jesus is revealing something important about how we relate to God. He employs the teaching method of compare and contrast which essentially says: if this is the case humanly speaking, how much more different with God. The unjust human judge says:

> . . .'Though I do not fear God nor regard man, yet
> because this widow troubles me I will avenge her,
> lest by her continual coming she weary (hupopiadzo)
> me.' (Luke 18:4-5, parentheses mine)

That word is used only once in the New Testament and has the figurative meaning 'to hit under the eye.' We would say this woman is constantly in his face. The point of the story is our willingness to go through the struggle, to be tenacious in faith, to hold on and even tussle with God, just as Jacob proved in his struggle with the preincarnate Son of God. In the Jewish mind, this is part of true relationship with the living God. That is, if you don't like the way things are going or you think justice is not being done on your behalf, tell God. If our view of God is that He is somehow distant and uninvolved, we won't do this.

This is a wonderful truth. Our modern 'instant gratification' lifestyle gets in the way of its daily application. We get discouraged when God doesn't execute judgment or answer prayer on our schedule. Faith seems to be the first casualty. Sometimes bitterness and the desire for revenge take its place. Instead, when things seem at their worst, we need to use prayer as a candle in the darkness.

Oswald Chambers wrote this motivating thought:

"Faith is the heroic effort of your life. You fling yourself in reckless confidence on God. God has ventured all in Jesus Christ to save us. Now, He wants us to venture our all in abandoned confidence in Him. Jesus Christ demands of the man who trusts Him the same reckless sporting spirit that the natural man exhibits. . .only one out of a crowd is daring enough to bank his faith on the character of God." (*My Utmost For His Highest, Classic Edition,* Oswald Chambers, copyright 1935, Dodd, Mead & Company, New York, Fifty-fourth printing, from May 8 and May 30 readings; public domain)

Theological arguments may have their place, but the fact remains that all people cross paths with trouble and pain at some point in their lives, and they search for answers and peace that we know only God can give. Living the example of trust in such a God may be the light (fotinos; see Matthew 5:14) that the unbelieving need to find their way to Him. The crux of the matter is this:

> *But without faith it is impossible to please Him, for*
> *he who comes to God must believe that He is and that*
> *He is a rewarder of those who diligently seek Him.*
> (Hebrews 11:6)

God delights in pure faith put in Him. Consider Jesus' pleasure in Abraham when he was about to sacrifice Isaac on Mount Moriah (the present-day site of the temple in Jerusalem). This is the kind of faith that God is looking for. When we whine about our circumstances or constantly question "Why?" we are not walking by the faith that makes Him stand up and take notice (humanly speaking).

When Paul writes of faith in Ephesians, he again uses military language, saying,

> *Above all, taking the shield of faith with which you*
> *will be able to quench all the fiery darts of the wicked*
> *one.* (Ephesians 6:16)

We all know that a shield is for protection in the battle. Early shields were made with animal hide stretched over a wooden frame. They were relatively light, but not of much value if the enemy used arrows with heads dipped in tar and lit on fire. You can see they would just burn up, leaving the warrior without protection. With advances in metallurgy, bronze shields were created that required more strength to carry, but a skillful fighter would endure the battle with it. Paul admonishes us about the figurative shield of faith to take its power seriously; *"above all,"* that is, even with the rest of your armor on, don't forget to take faith with you always. Faith is our first line of defense against the attacks of the enemy. True, we have the helmet of salvation, but faith came first. So why does God seem to always test our faith? I think it is because in doing so, we learn to raise the shield, strengthening that muscle so it doesn't atrophy.

The fact is that our faith in God is always being tested by this world system, what it thinks of us and of our God. You never arrive at a place where your faith is adequate. It will be tested until the day you draw your last breath. You will need a tested and tried and strong faith when you endure a prolonged trial in your life, such as the desert experience.

I am going to venture something here that is not unreasonable regarding faith. In Matthew 17, the disciples come to Jesus perplexed that they could not heal a boy experiencing seizures. A little word study is helpful here to understand the seriousness of the situation. His condition is described in the NKJV as that of an epileptic, but the King James version uses the word 'lunatic' (derived from lunar, pertaining to the moon). This is because the original Greek word is s*eleniazomai* – from Selene, the Greek moon goddess. Selenite is a rock from which the element selenium is derived. According to Webster, the rock was thought, at one time, to change in luster with the brightness of the moon. We all have a trace amount of the element in our bodies, and it has been found to be essential to our health. Interestingly, it is found concentrated in desert river deltas such as the Colorado River after it has completed its journey to California, having been depleted for irrigation along the way.

To explain this passage by our modern psychology, the young man in the story might be bipolar, a mental disease that is associated with a change in moods, i.e., from cheerfulness to depression without any rational cause. In this case, it caused him to do harmful, even suicidal things to himself. The boy's father was clearly frustrated by the disciples' inability to bring healing. Jesus acted in a manner that revealed the cause to be demonic. In other words, some matters require exercising faith by means of prayer and fasting, two practices that are intended to remind us of the need for greater reliance on God to solve the problem.

In the gospel of Matthew, Jesus says

> *If you have faith as a mustard seed, you will say to this mountain, 'Move from here to there,' and it will move; and nothing will be impossible for you.* (Matthew 17:20)

This could have been spoken by Jesus as he stood across the valley from the Herodium—a pleasure palace built by Herod the Great around 40 – 15 BC. It was built within a tall earthwork mound, the dirt for which is said to have been moved from a location on the other side of the valley. It is easily the width of three football fields at its base. In an era without modern earth moving equipment, it would have been considered a marvel at the time of its construction. Indeed, present day archeological digs show the immensity of the project. Yet it was accomplished by moving dirt and rock a little at a time. Isn't this sometimes true of faith? We see God working on our behalf a little at a time as we wait on Him.

In using the mustard seed analogy, Jesus may have been saying that faith does, indeed, start small but it can grow to the strength of literally moving mountains. The mustard seed analogy is also used in three of the gospels where the seed eventually becomes the size of a small tree that can literally support birds. From my own experience with desert weeds like the kochia that I have battled on my own land, the analogy works. This weed has many tiny seeds. At germination, it is very small and difficult to distinguish. All it takes is a little water, though, and its growth is exponential! One summer, we were away from the place for only two weeks and came back to find these weeds taller than me in an area where irrigation was poorly managed by the neighboring farmer. They were now beyond the capability of most farm equipment to deal with, so it took many hours of hard labor to cut them down, stack, and burn them. In the meantime, guess who benefitted? The quail population exploded that fall from all the shelter that started with just tiny seeds.

My point here is that you need to cultivate a stronger faith to see greater things done. Combining this with the previous parable, manmade mountains are built at great expense of labor and energy. Likewise, a growing faith comes through the exercise of it.

Hope

I have already used the word hope many times up to this point. After all, it is one of the three that endure in the great love chapter of 1 Corinthians, so it must hold a place of great importance to the believer. But what is it? We should not gloss over it. Without hope, the desert dweller would give up the struggle and let the wild beasts devour her. John Bunyan wrote, "Hope is not ill if faith is well," perhaps meaning that if our trust in God is healthy, we can experience this thing called hope. It has also been said that hope is the oxygen of the soul. Have you ever experienced a time of hopelessness in your life? What do people need in times of hopelessness? One thing I can say without hesitation is encouragement. They need courage to go on when their reservoir of courage is drained. People in trouble need reminders of the pleasant things in life because it gives them hope. It is good when brotherly love includes healing salve on the wounds. This is where mere words will not do. Maybe that is feet on the ground getting someone settled into a new home after they have suffered a debilitating health problem. Or it might be reminding someone you are still praying for them.

Having said that, it is interesting that the New Testament speaks of hope in an entirely different way. The context is never about our circumstances in life. Rather, it is always about the hope of our resurrection in Christ finally being realized. This is how I believe our God would have us view our times of hopelessness, making our true hope especially relevant in the desert. It is in looking at a future resurrection that our spirits get their ultimate boost. Looking to Christ our redeemer lifts us like nothing or no person could ever do! This is the anchor of the soul that we read about in Hebrews 6.

Do you think that dreaming of financial security can build hope in your dire circumstances? Even that would be temporary. Paul writes,

Hope that is seen is not hope. (Romans 8:24)

That makes sense. If we could see the future perfectly, there would be no need for this thing called hope.

But if we hope for what we do not see, then we eagerly wait for it with perseverance. (Romans 8:25)

The best vision we have now is seeing *"in a mirror dimly,"* (*esoptron* - think 'optics' as in reading glasses; 1 Corinthians 13:12). The word dimly is interesting (*ainigma*). From it, we get our word enigma. An enigma is something hard to explain or understand, even a riddle. This is the way of life so often. We can't explain why things happen to us the way they do. And the future is a complete riddle that we figure out as we go ahead in life by faith rather than sight (2 Corinthians 5:7).

And what is the biblical definition of faith? It *"is the substance of things hoped for,"* (Hebrews 11:1). We have come full circle now. This 'substance' is *hupostasis* in the original; stasis is the condition of standing still and hupo, as previously noted, is a prefix meaning 'under' (see chapter 3 and the similar topic about faith and trials). To put it in an analogy that only a civil engineer could love, it is like a bridge spanning a body of water. All bridges are stationary unless they are moved by wind forces. The decks are supported by girders. Ultimately, the loads they carry are delivered to foundations under water. We use them to get from one side of a body of water to the other. Thus it is when we trust God across the journey of life. It is the conviction that things you can't see are really there (i.e., the person of God or heaven). This is an important reality that the desert journeyer needs to survive the trek.

Happiness

To this point, I have not said much about happiness. In America, we give this an exalted position. It is even enshrined in our Declaration of Independence. The word 'happy' is translated as such in the New Testament only seven times and has the meaning of being fortunate. The Old Testament has just a few more usages than that. Joy and rejoicing are used many more times. I think this is largely because we are instructed from our ancient manuscripts to live always in a state of rejoicing rather than seek happiness which can come and go with our fortunes or friendships. That doesn't mean there is anything wrong or sinful about happiness. Human happiness is valuable because we are created with emotions that are satisfied by it. We all prefer to be happy than sad. We work hard to avoid sadness, even denying its unwelcome presence from time to time (perhaps by consuming chocolate or ice cream as an antidote).

Young adults make up a large part of those who use Facebook and other contemporary social media sites. A research survey revealed that the more often this demographic used Facebook, the less happy they felt. The research concluded that millennials today resort to posting their sadness online or by message on their phones and spend inordinate amounts of time on social media just to get affirmation from their friends. It was discovered that their brains actually release endorphins from this and that these people are addicted to the feeling or "high" that they get from that activity. The result is a loss of processing and truly understanding our feelings, thinking through things and creatively solving our problems. (Facebook Use Predicts Declines in Subjective Well-Being in Young Adults, University of Michigan, August 14, 2013; https://doi.org/10.1371/journal.pone; accessed January 31, 2020). One conclusion we can reach from this is that social media does not fully satisfy our need for human companionship and affirmation.

There is a biblical understanding of happiness, though. For example, 'rejoice' in Philippians. 3:1 is translated from *chairo* and has the meaning of being calmly happy or cheerful. It is the root of *charis*, translated throughout the New Testament as 'grace.' You can see that biblical happiness is a choice and action that has nothing to do with our circumstances. Still, the matter of happiness as it relates to the desert experience deserves some attention because the person in that time of life pines for it, even while trying to exercise the discipline of rejoicing.

A sociological study at the University of Minnesota found that most happiness results from genetics and life events. The latter are things that occurred in the recent past, but their impact on happiness doesn't last long (for example, getting married and then finding that the real work of maintaining the marriage has just begun). A mere 12 percent comes from four things, but they are compelling because they are totally within our control (*A Formula For Happiness*, Arthur C. Brooks, December 14, 2013, American Enterprise Institute website, aei.org, accessed January 11, 2020):

- A theological framework to make sense of death and suffering; a world view that can explain where you are in time and space.
- Family – people in your home that love you.
- Community – just two or three friends that have an expansive sense of the self, such that when you are happy, they are too; when you hurt, they are sad. Without these, we experience loneliness.
- Work – do I think it matters? Am I needed? What is the nature of your work? This is the biggest of the four. As a matter of fact, unemployment proves catastrophic for happiness.

As for the last one in the list (work), most men will attest to it because we are driven to find purpose in what we do for a living. When that is gone or when we leave it either involuntarily or through retirement, a chunk of our happiness is missing unless it can be filled by a new line of work or volunteering or (may I suggest) expanding our horizons for the Kingdom of God.

Pertaining to the third one listed, anecdotal surveys have revealed that real friendships as described are declining—even down to 1.5 persons now. Here, I think it is important to qualify the meaning of true friendship. It isn't the five-minute conversation with someone every Sunday after church. With that, you may become well-acquainted, but you are not good friends. In friendship, there is some sharing of everyday normal life.

When in the desert long enough, we begin to feel that we are drying up. And your fear from this is friendships that took years to cultivate and were so sweet may never be back again in this life. Lasting friendships are hard to come by. People nowadays are less willing to commit to relationships of that sort because it involves too much risk. So much energy is invested in raising children and building friendships; when those people are no longer connecting with us, some of our will is drained. You think the solution is to try to hang on to them, but you are a desert dweller and those people are not there. Nor can they come there.

Though within our control, happiness from family and friends is subject to what I would call relationship entropy—the degradation of its usefulness. But with proper maintenance, it is kept going. My rule is that friendship is a two-way street, so it is just as much my responsibility to maintain that bond as it is my friend's. Truth be told, some life events that give us temporary happiness can continue to provide happiness if we put some additional effort into them, marriage being the most obvious example.

There is a biblical principal regarding friendship that I think has received scant attention. The word *phileo* is used several times in our New Testament and is translated as "love" for us English speakers. Here is my take on it. Going a little deeper, *phileo* can mean friendship, sentimental attachment, or personal relation. In Paul's first letter to the Corinthian Church, he uses it in a stern warning: "If anyone does not love the Lord Jesus Christ, let him be accursed." (1 Corinthians 16:22) In essence, he is saying you must have a personal relationship with Christ. Nothing else will do!

But he uses the same word in his letter to Titus.

Greet those who phileo us in the faith. (Titus 3:15)

To the Christian I ask, are you just friendly, or do you have genuine friendships with your fellow believers? When you love someone in that manner, you provide an important part of their emotional needs. We often think of sentimentality as frivolous. But we all have carted around keepsakes and family heirlooms for decades because they mean something to us, and we just can't jettison them. Shouldn't it be much more so with our friendships? Take the risk and try it.

In fact, where do we get the notion that we don't need one another, especially in the Church? We are prone to neglect hospitality over the pettiest differences. I think the persecuted

Church abroad gets this better because they have learned through trial by fire that they desperately need each other.

CHAPTER 5

LIVING WITH LONELINESS AND ISOLATION

The last thing I will touch on as experienced in the desert (though certainly not least) is the sense of isolation and loneliness one feels sometimes. Even in an age of information overload via social media, we still experience loneliness and sadness. I can't speak for my entire generation, but I tend not to spend much time on social media, even though I freely acknowledge its value and that of modern communication technology in keeping up with friends and family where hundreds and even thousands of miles separate us. But it strikes me that it can become idolatrous when we are pulled away from the closeness that God wants with us, all the while believing that the presence of people can satisfy our deepest longings more than He.

Isolation

It's one thing to be despised by your enemies. You expect that. David's enemies were of the military kind; those who were seeking to kill him. I don't have those (that I am aware of anyway). But I've had some who wanted to harm my reputation, and that is enough of an enemy for me. It is enough of an enemy for anyone. Where it really hurts, though, is when friends and family seem to distance themselves from you. Proverbs 27:10 has this to say:

Do not forsake your own friend or your father's friend.

I think God is telling us something of the value of friendship, especially when life gets hard. Are you among those who experience the perplexity of people in your circle who are supposed to love you but seemingly forget all about you for years? This is now called "ghosting." It is a desert experience. When your efforts are ignored or, worse, commitments of "let's get together soon" are forgotten, it dampens your morale. There can also be a sense of *stenochoria* that we reviewed in chapter 3. That is, you feel the canyon walls closing in on you as your friends forsake you one by one for no apparent reason.

During times when my joblessness was prolonged, we noticed that friends in the church would only talk to us about that. It was good that they were concerned, especially when they told us they were praying. Most of them were not out of work. One thing we came to understand is that people are not one-dimensional. In a crisis, they are still in need of social contact, love, and acceptance. When that is missing, an unwarranted shame creeps in as they wonder if something is wrong with them. Now I am not foolish enough to think that life does not happen to them as well. In fact, we found in time that some were experiencing pain from wayward children or hardship from health problems. About the beginning of my desert time, one of our friends was hurt badly in an ATV accident. We knew nothing about it, which is no credit to us, though we certainly would like to have been there for them when it happened. But when friendships fade away, you sometimes feel banished for no apparent reason other than your adverse circumstances in life.

The desert dweller is especially inclined toward a feeling of diminishment in the eyes of others. We clamor for any proof that life is not passing us by, so we look for satisfaction in the next dollar earned and spent, the next great relationship or the next adventure in life. In a cynical way, we think the abundance of people around us (perhaps a busy social schedule) shows God's seal of approval on our lives and that, without it, He is somehow signaling that something is wrong with us. So, we try harder to make friends and relatives like us only to see them become more cold and distant, perhaps even pushing us away or ignoring us for long stretches. What we are really doing is clamoring for a way out of the desert when what God wants is the isolation that drives us to Him alone. It is difficult to convince our desperate minds of the sufficiency of the triune God. God in three persons should be entirely satisfying to us! In other words, I think God is calling us in the desert for the purpose of cultivating a deeper friendship with Him instead of people. Can we get it through our heads that God longs for us to long for Him?

The children of Israel left their bondage in Egypt (which I might argue was truly the desert of their days, but it doesn't work as well metaphorically) with friends and family together. Presumably, then, their experience didn't include loss of friendships. The ruling class of the day was largely responsible for their misery as slaves. Even so, many Egyptians sent them on their way with valuables as well as necessities since they had *"gained favor in the sight of the Egyptians . . . "* (Exodus 12:36). You would think the freedom purchased by God would have cemented their allegiance to Him. But when Moses left to hear all the instructions from God on the mountains of Sinai, their fears and insecurities returned and they sought comfort by frantically collecting these trinkets, melting them, and forming an idol to worship. They asked Aaron to make gods.

I think even in our own deserts, we too, can become frantic, believing that we need to do something about our situation because a word from the Lord has been absent for a while. Wright addresses this by saying:

"We are people who tend toward idolatry. We create idols and build our lives around them. For many, the body and how it looks is an idol. For some, wealth and possessions are idols. And for many, whether they realize it or not, their work is an idol. When something becomes everything to us, that is idolatry."

(Recovering from Losses in Life, H. Norman Wright, copyright 1991, republished 2006, Fleming H. Revell Co., p 137)

In life's deserts, you feel afraid because the bonds of human kinship seem to have unraveled, but this is the very time to be calm, take your bearings and worship God in truth and spirit.

In Psalm 71, the writer seems to have both observed his plight of isolation and realized the true antidote. I think he was experiencing dehumanization from those around him when he says

I have become as a wonder to many. (Psalm 71:7)

My own experience with this comes from the workplace at those times when a business is struggling. Everyone knows it. And those around you who have the best connections start zeroing in on your faults and short-comings mostly behind your back. For some, it might be by applying labels to tarnish your reputation. These are all signs they realize their piece of the pie is threatened, that lean times are coming.

David may have been referring to the kind of people who must dehumanize others to protect themselves. If they succeed, it is easier to cut them loose and forget about them. I felt the sting of it on one occasion when a supervisor questioned the validity of my professional credentials to my face. It came out of his mouth unexpectedly and was galling to hear. I worked hard for my professional license and passed all the required exams. But to people who want to hurt you, none of that matters. It's all about survival in this world system though it reveals a kind of soullessness. It is part of being made a 'wonder,' a sort of out-of-place thing. In seeing this, the writer of the psalm makes several pleas to God:

Do not forsake me when my strength fails (vs. 9b)

My enemies speak against me (vs. 10a)

Those who lie in wait for my life take counsel together (vs. 10b – this could mean "circling the wagons" to threaten someone's livelihood)

When I am old and grayheaded, O God, do not forsake me (vs. 18)

This truly is the cry of an older man in the desert experience of life, who may be finally realizing the great truth that it is more important for one to walk into the sunset of life close by the Lord's side. Even in saying,

O God, who is like You? You, who have shown me great and severe troubles . . . (vs. 19-20)

he sees the purpose:

Let my mouth be filled with Your praise and with Your glory all the day. (vs. 8a)

I will hope continually, and will praise You yet more and more. (vs. 14)

I will go in the strength of the Lord GOD. (vs. 16a)

I will make mention of Your righteousness. (vs. 16b)

My lips shall greatly rejoice when I sing to You. (vs. 23a)

These are the words of a person who has seen that the desert times of being undermined by people are meant to drive us into a deeper relationship with the one who has "*. . . given the commandment to save me,*" (vs. 3).

My wife and I experienced what I refer to as the vagabond years from our late 40s to our early 60s. In a small way, we could relate to what military families experience moving from one base to another throughout their career. In that time, I had four different employers, lived in six different dwellings and three towns. One of the first things we committed ourselves to doing in a new community was finding a church that met three criteria: 1) we felt welcome by the leadership, 2) the members were friendly, and 3) it was a place where we could be involved in kingdom-building ministry of some kind. It isn't as easy to find as you might think.

Usually, we spent the better part of the first year visiting churches before we settled on one where we believed God wanted us. In Moses Lake, we talked to one woman whose family had been involved in the church and community for over twenty years, and she confided with some perplexity her observation that it takes seven or eight years to get established and accepted there. She agreed with us—that is too long. In most cases, we found that people were friendly in the lobby, but not willing to form friendships with those perceived as short timers. We learned that most people will not invest their lives in desert vagabonds.

In time, God dealt with me about a purpose of isolation in life's deserts. Here is a verse expressive of the desperate dryness of the desert.

As the deer pants for the water brooks, so pants my soul
for You. (Psalm 42:1)

The Sons of Korah who wrote this are not saying the soul longs for more friends, but more of God—a deeper friendship with God, if you will. While we find it uncomfortable to embrace that fully, it is impossible to know him intimately without being alone with him in the arid places of human existence. We tend to think when we are surrounded by friends and family and the tide is not against us that we are experiencing blessing because of our closeness to God. If we think that family desertion is a sign of judgment from God, it probably isn't. He sometimes sweeps our earthly relationships aside for a while so we can see Him more clearly. I think David understood this when he tells God that he is in trouble and needs help:

I am a reproach among all my enemies,
But especially among my neighbors,
And am repulsive to my acquaintances;
Those who see me outside flee from me.
I am forgotten like a dead man, out of mind;
I am like a broken vessel.
For I hear the slander of many; fear is on every side;
...But as for me, I trust in You, O LORD;
I say, 'You are my God.' (Psalm 31:11-14)

A final word on this – when you find that an accounting of your prayers and supplications show they are not being answered by God, you truly experience the loneliness and isolation of feeling like even <u>He</u> isn't around. But it is a deceptive feeling. Be careful about getting too comfortable with it. I have been told by well-meaning Christians that it is sign that one has unconfessed sin. Here, I am not saying that we shouldn't check ourselves for that condition, but it isn't necessarily the heart of the matter. Our Father in heaven still wants us to seek Him in the silent times.

Loneliness

Underlying all of this is the growing sense of loneliness. It is a part of the desert experience for many people, even when surrounded by others. Sometimes, it feels like people are not even aware of your existence; at the very least, you feel ignored. After all, people move on with their lives even when yours seems to be standing still. From the stage of life, it looks like there is no audience except a few hecklers. It is tempting to fight this with self-reliance or to seek the affirmation of people. If either of those don't work, you lose confidence and a nagging fear starts to surround unless you cry out to God and ask Him to be your constant companion. Support from people is a good thing, but we tend to rely on it too much. The Lord may be using a season like this because He wants us all to Himself. Paradoxically, no one else is with you in the desert . .

. except the God who made you. I am not saying that you are the only one going through the desert experience. There are many others, but it seems like you are alone until you grasp that God is there and desires fellowship with you and worship from you.

Loneliness sometimes prompts introspection to our harm. For example, it might cause us to struggle with which side of the line blame falls on for our problems in life. Is it because of our sin or is it just because God is refining us? Jesus addressed this question with the disciples when they asked it regarding the man blind from birth (John 9:2). In fact, sin wasn't involved at all. It was the plan of God to show His mighty power through the revealed Messiah. Our temptation is to drift toward thinking that the wilderness is for punishment—a place to which we are banished instead of what it really is—the place where God is calling us to be satisfied in Him alone. It might even be that place where He shows His mighty hand through your most humbling circumstances.

I experienced many days of loneliness during my prolonged joblessness from the 2009-2011 Depression. To stay engaged, I started working my small patch of land in western Idaho near the Snake River while looking for full-time paying work. Throughout this preoccupation, I got to spend many hours plugged into my trusty MP3 player listening to music and some sermons that took me into a deeper application of God's Word. In fact, His Word was beginning to make more sense during these trials than at any other time. It was forming anchors to keep me close to my God while on a desert journey that I still could not understand without in some way thinking it was punishment for sins past . . . or whatever. I would also spend long hours in prayer. In the end, these lessons were the real fruit I got off the land considering that the rest of my effort turned into a battle with . . . weeds. Since this can easily be turned into a metaphor on life, I will do so.

My immediate goal was to plant some pasture grass to keep the weeds out. Part of the reason for doing this was just to keep the dream alive. Thankfully, my wife encouraged me to do it because she wisely considered that a man needs purpose and focus or he will get discouraged; worse, he may give up. I put a great deal of physical energy into it, attempting to tame the land with simple gardening tools and some jury-rigged devices. Some days I would be there 10 hours, trying to make the most of a 60-mile round trip from our house. It was a lonely endeavor. In time, my wife and I also established the axiom that life wins in the countryside . . . every time. Gophers, weeds, insects, mice, and you name it—you are always fighting them for control. In the midst of it all, you see some amazing things in God's created order.

I hatched a plan to prepare three acres of our land for irrigation. Prior to this, we had simply leased the land to a farmer. They carve shallow troughs in the soil (a process known as corrugating) with an implement 20 feet wide pulled through loose soil by a large tractor. I had neither so I jury-rigged a device using some lumber and scrap metal parts attached to the front of my old burned-out lawn mower that I planned to push through the soil three rows at a time. But before I could do that, I had to remove what appeared to be a few weeds. I soon discovered that there were also clumps of leftover roots from the previous fall's corn crop hidden beneath the surface and getting in the way of progress.

The job looked doable at first, but I wasn't there every day. Summer sun and a little moisture from a late wet spring showed me how fast weeds can grow. While I was working on the upper portion of ground, the lower was literally being overwhelmed with weeds of at least six different species, some more difficult to remove than others and some that grew quickly to the size I believe Jesus was talking about in His parable about the kingdom of God and the mustard seed. It didn't help that the previous year the farmer who was renting our land had applied a generous amount of cow manure from the nearby dairy. Wow!

At this point, I saw the need to change tactics and quickly tame the lower portion while the weeds still seemed manageable. Bring on the rototiller—not your garden variety tiller, but the biggest one I could find from the local rental business. This one came with its own trailer. I picked it up early one morning and worked practically non-stop for 12 hours, taking only short breaks until nearly dark that day. I was surprised to learn how much area one can till in that amount of time (about a third of an acre) and yet how little difference it made. The work before me was daunting, and I still had not planted any grass. I am sure the farmers driving by were shaking their heads in disbelief by now.

My strategy had to shift to weed control, if not to keep them from spreading, to at least save myself the embarrassment of a field covered with nothing but weeds next to the neighboring fields of grain. Time for one of the greatest inventions for the farmer . . . Roundup®. I made some rudimentary calculations on the quantity I would need to knock down all these weeds and bought two gallons of the stuff. Diluted properly, it would cover two acres, and the container came with a little hand wand. Though it was the poor man's method for spraying (remember, I am out of work and my unemployment compensation ran out months earlier), I found it was slow and labor intensive, almost like applying it with a squirt gun. I had to run back and forth to mix and fill the next batch in the container every 30 minutes or so. Then, the spray nozzle would clog repeatedly with whatever small piece of grit or weed got into the spray container. This required pressuring down the container, removing the nozzle, cleaning it with a paper clip and repressuring again. I learned to be very careful to keep small contaminants out of the container.

I finally got the upper portion of the land in good enough shape, I thought, to do a planting of grass seed. I thought all along that this could be done easily with a hand-held rotary distributor, the one I used all the time to scatter fertilizer on the lawn. But I found out that the mix of pasture grass seed I purchased would not go through the bottom opening of the spreader at any setting. It didn't matter how much shaking you did to 'fluff' it up. It simply would not flow because the seeds would become intertwined. Well, the rain clouds were gathering that day, and I didn't want to miss the opportunity for some germination to take place, so I resorted to the biblical method of casting seed by hand from a bucket. As luck would have it, the wind had picked up enough to make that method uncontrollable. I pressed on and managed to seed about a fourth of an acre, raked it around and hoped for the best. I had not turned any irrigation on to it. I couldn't . . . not until I had channeled a way for the water to reach the bottom of the property. A few weeks later, there was germination, all right—a second generation of weeds. No grass. For this, the preacher of Ecclesiastes has the words, *"Vanity of vanities, all is vanity."* It was the beginning of realizing that farming of any kind was going to be hard work, especially without the proper equipment.

By the third week of June, I was battling weeds that were chest high along the north side of the parcel. In most other places, they were waist high. With added manpower from my wife on a couple of Saturdays, we managed to get an application of Roundup® over the entire property and it was working. One thing you learn, though, is that herbicides don't work overnight, especially on mature weeds. On these, it can take up to two weeks to kill them. Though I had beaten them, I was left with tall stands that needed to be reduced to mulch and plowed under before I could plant grass. At this point, my strength was drained and the continued discouragement of my joblessness did not improve my morale. I was discovering that working the land was not a one-man job and certainly not one to be accomplished with mere hand tools.

Now, I could go into how this is a metaphor for that and means this, but that's straining a bit to make a point. Let's keep the metaphors to a minimum. One thing is for sure, though. You are reminded that desert life is at times a struggle, fighting to keep the problems under control and trying to keep things in the perspective of kingdom living; in particular, not being anxious about the things of this life. They can explode out of control and, no matter the effort to try corralling them, you discover it can't be done in your strength alone. Others possess power that you have no control over. All you can do is live your life, run your race (Hebrews 12:1). And finally . . . farming is hard work. Did I already mention that?

Even in the lonesomeness of desert existence, I don't think that all our human relationships are meant to be sacrificed. After all, God created us to live in relationship to one another. While I believe it is important for others to recognize this need, most often, they will not. It is also possible that when people only relate to you on the level of your crisis, you become defined by that. People might avoid you because of that.

But the apostle Paul gives commands that are important and helpful for the health of the church body.

> *We, being many, are one body in Christ, and individually members of one another.* (Romans 12:5)

Yes, that includes those enduring the deserts of life. I have already said that those people are the first to be forgotten because the place they inhabit is inhospitable to others. However, Paul isn't just giving advice. He goes on to command things that are particularly the role of the church in ministering to the body. If you don't know how to encourage someone in the desert, start here:

> *Be kindly affectionate* (philostorgos) *to one another with brotherly love* (philadelphia), *in honor giving preference* (prohegeomai) *to one another.* (Romans 12:10)

You see two of the four forms of love in the Greek language here. *Storge* refers to cherishing of natural relations—a fondness for family. The second is the familiar brotherly love.

Of course, the context of this chapter is the church body, so we are to see one another as family. You obviously treat family differently than mere friends. It is a more intimate form of love. The verse says we are to do this by proactively honoring one another (think again of the military term "hegemony," as if moving in assertively). I think he used such strong language to get our attention.

And one more thing:

> *Be of the same mind toward one another.* (Romans 12:16a)

I used to read this verse as trying to reconcile our differences of opinion but have come to understand a more likely interpretation as that of being interested in one another. After all, no one agrees about everything, and we aren't to think that our opinions matter more than the opinions of others. But we should make an effort to show interest in our brothers and sisters, what they are going through and truly listen when that may be all they really need from you. Remember, the person in the desert is going through a very humbling time in one sense. God is directing His people to see that and spend some quality time with them. Perhaps a good rule of thumb would be 'kindness first' because you don't know what difficulties people in your sphere will be facing down the road in a month or a year or even ten years. We usually don't regret the kindnesses we expend on others.

I learned in my desert years that the work of job hunting is a lonely experience . . . and mostly unfruitful. In the 2009 depression, I tried all the conventional methods, and some unconventional, to find a place back in my profession. Some people have enough contacts that networking quickly results in finding people who need your skill and like you well enough on first impression. I didn't have more than a handful at the time so I tried using a firm that advertised itself as a career placement business with a unique system for developing your contacts, thereby increasing your chances for finding a job—nothing spectacular there. In fact, I doubted they could teach me much I didn't already know. They also promised to start you off with some already established contact lists in your area of endeavor. When I paid their fee and began looking over their lists, my disappointment was palpable. Many of the names were out of date and some of the companies had gone out of business. But it wasn't a complete loss. For one thing, it forced me to interact with people on a regular basis and to sharpen my communication skills.

The whole process of looking for work as a professional is also humbling. But even in a lonely effort like this, we can cling to a lesson from Psalm 139:17-18. God thinks about us. Not just once in the morning as we do with Him but throughout every day of our lives and into the night. It's a good thing, I think, to just thank God at least once during the day for thinking about us. And they are not thoughts of malice. Our human relationships seem so fragile, but our relationship with God will never be that way. He promised that.

Just one more anecdote. Even the friends who stay with you in the desert can't last forever. Some might say it's silly to interject this thought, but I must give a little tribute to our cocker spaniel that we laid to rest in the spring of 2013 after 15 years of companionship. Pets don't consider you an inconvenience, and they can certainly offer soothing comfort, as did this dog. We took her almost everywhere, but the thing I remember most was her joining me at the desk as I forged through the lonely and discouraging process of job hunting in my mid-fifties when practically no person would stop by for months on end. She was a faithful friend, just doing what God had designed her for in one of life's dry spells. The only time pets break your heart is when they die. OK, enough said about that (sniff).

Family and the Desert

The unwelcome times of family alienation are intruders in your desert experience. I observed this when a family member, down on his luck (also affected by the economic depression of 2009), was visiting our dad. He had agreed to let this family member and his wife stay with him for a while. I discerned a very real sense of loss in this man as his dreams and livelihood were crushed in the place he had lived for many years. By my assessment, this was indeed a desert time for him.

My dad lost his wife only two years prior to that and was dealing with loneliness. My wife and I witnessed this first-hand when we arranged a surprise visit in the winter just after he had been released from the local hospital. When we walked in the door, he was sitting in one of the old living room chairs, bundled in a blanket with the thermostat set to below 60 degrees! We could see it was a kind of depression creeping in. Like most parents, it was my dad's desire to live independently in his home if practical. His was a rather large old farmhouse on two acres, so there was too much for one old man to maintain. Having someone there was a good thing in one sense as it provided what my dad most wanted until his dying day.

Unfortunately, there were some unintended consequences from this arrangement that later erupted in family discord. It involved the shenanigans many families endure in handling their parents' estate. What should be discussed in the open sunshine is, instead, done without other siblings' knowledge. It sometimes involves manipulation of parents not in their right mind and perhaps a shady lawyer. Other family members feel defrauded. Wounds fester, communication breaks down and people start avoiding one another because of the hurt. I was unprepared when it happened in our family. Life gets complicated. Through this episode, I came to understand that this is exactly what all of us are capable of doing as sinners, so I shouldn't be surprised.

This happened in the midst of my own desert experience and revealed sibling rivalry that was once only a part of our childhood. The adult version is worse because it is fueled by envy over perceived status, position, and power in life without acknowledging that we all suffer pain and disappointment from which our money and possessions cannot deliver us. Knowing now that this is part of the desert experience, I also realize you can't blame yourself for everything that goes wrong in a relationship.

That is really an abbreviated summary for the purpose of showing just how desert can deepen through the fracturing of family relationships and the loss of support from friends. It helps illustrate the brokenness encountered along the way from acts that are not well thought out for their consequences (family relationships strained at the very least and completely broken at worst). Only God can mend what has been done. And His way is through the heart first.

It has also been helpful for me to learn (too late in life, I think) why tone is so important in our communication. People are so easily offended. It is our default mode. Don't let it be that way. That is, don't let it be your first reaction to something a person says to you. I am not implying that someone else's bad tone should be excused. But try to hear and not be hurt. People are notoriously bad communicators because of our selfish, sinful nature.

One thing that has helped me through this comes from 1 Corinthians, the end of chapter 3, where Paul has instructed the church regarding their preference for certain persons over others in the faith. In a deeper sense, I think the Word of God here speaks about what we think of others and what they think of us. When he speaks of all things being ours (vs. 21), including things that happen now or in the future or what we gain from those who teach us, it doesn't matter what others say about us or think about us because, in Christ, God isn't showing partiality. It doesn't matter what we think of others. It follows, then, that it doesn't matter what others think of us.

Paul alludes to this in 1 Corinthians chapter 4. The important thing is that others see us as servants of Christ and stewards of the mysteries of God. The word used for minister or servant in 4:1 comes from *huperetes*. Used just twice in the New Testament, this is the term for an under-rower (remember, huper = under). Paul was familiar with this term perhaps from his many travels over the Mediterranean Sea. These were galley slaves (two or three decks below the main deck) whose job was to power the ships—a large contingent of men rowing the ship into battle or against the storm. You can imagine it was the most arduous of tasks, literally straining at the oars. They were often left to die in the event the ship was sunk. Now, our Lord would not do this to us, but Paul wants to connect the reader to how we should see ourselves in service to Christ; we are to put all things in submission to Him no matter the suffering we face. We are no longer in control.

God taught me a lesson about this through an interaction with my own son and the natural world. Earlier in this book, I wrote about a trip we took together into the wilderness of northeast Oregon. This event took place several years before I was even contemplating a book on the desert of life, but I believe God was using it to prepare my heart and mind for things to come. After we set up camp at our destination, my son began to speak about a change of direction in his life. He knew I would try to talk him out of it. I could see and hear how resolved he was in the matter, and I realized then it was the main reason he wanted to do this trek with me. First, he knew I loved the wilderness experience. Second, he had me all to himself for this important message. I give him credit for setting the stage properly for my receptiveness. If he had just given me the news over the phone or, worse yet, in a text message, I would certainly have been angry and bitter over it.

But there in the silent, starlit night around a campfire, we could talk—man to man. There wasn't any getting away from each other.

I sat and listened as he told me he was dropping out of college after finishing this, his fifth year—just a semester shy of his degree. I don't remember all that was said, but we spoke as gentlemen. I felt a tinge of failure on my part at not being able to help him over the final hurdle. I knew it was a life-changing decision on his part. So, yes, I went to bed more than a little disappointed.

The next morning, we were awakened by some buzzing outside our small tent. I got up to do the morning camp routine and get the fire going. Upon returning, the buzzing was now inside our tent. To our astonishment, it was a hummingbird that had somehow flown inside. Believe it or not, this tiny creature is often curious of humans and will hover within feet of your face to observe. It is as if God is giving you the opportunity to look and behold for a moment His intricate design. This one was trapped and we could tell did not know how to find the door. It flew around inside, panicked I am sure. This went on for ten minutes as we tried to help the tiny bird, being careful not to injure it. But we otherwise had no control. All we could do was open the flap, let the bird see daylight and eventually find its own way out.

We were both surprised and delighted having a front row seat for this drama. When it finally found the exit, a life lesson almost immediately dawned on me. Our children, too, will find themselves in circumstances where they feel trapped. Change has come. There is clarity and peace in realizing when you no longer have control over your children's' lives. When that time comes, you must let go so they can find their own way. It isn't easy because you know their choices have consequences. Still, you must relinquish control. Amazingly, God sent this tiny messenger to teach an important lesson to me in a setting where he had my attention. It was what I needed most at the time.

My wife has a schefflera plant (botanical name schefflera arboricola) that has been with us now for 40 years. It was a little potted plant when her mother gave it to her after I slipped an engagement ring on her finger. It is almost like a family member. Now, at 6 feet tall and just as wide, it has survived without trying. We have moved it a dozen times from house to house in our wanderings. It is fascinating to watch through the seasons as it goes dormant in the winter and turns its leaves in unison toward the window in earnest seeking for sunlight to fuel its life cycle. Then, several times throughout the year, it sprouts tiny clusters of leaves while old ones die off and fall to the floor. We have repotted it many times, thinking each time that it would not survive the shock. Still, it lives on. It does not toil or spin (as in the making of clothes to survive). It has no mind. God created it to do just what it has been doing while teaching us the lesson that our God is completely reliable to keep us going until that day we are called home to Him forever.

He is faithful. I have come to understand the attribute of God we call faithfulness means that He never gives up on us. This is what Jesus meant when He said, *"I will never leave you, nor forsake you."* After some time in the desert, you learn that God is faithful, no matter your circumstances. This is a lesson that you must experience and learn from.

Old schefflera next to what it would look like in 1979 (on the table at the right).

CHAPTER 6

HELP FOR THE DESERT DWELLER

We all know the difference between book learning and real-life experience. My engineering education dealt largely with theory of structural design, fluid systems, physics, and materials science. The textbooks tried to throw some 'real world' problems at us. When I took my first job, I had the privilege of applying the academic world to problem solving with actual steel and concrete, sometimes in situations that required imagination and creativity. We must also apply the learning we get from the pages of Scripture to real life. We can discuss, study, and debate it; nothing wrong with that. But there comes a time where the rubber meets the desert road, and whatever we have studied and perhaps memorized gets tested in the day to day.

Running Well

In chapter 3, we covered loss as suffering - from Paul's letter to the church at Philippi. It is important to add here that Paul instructs us to count <u>all things</u> loss, even the things that are <u>not</u> gain. James 3:2 says we all stumble in <u>many</u> things (not the least in what we say). That is, we have many failures. So, if we don't leave failure behind, we will be hamstrung in the race. About the worst kind of injury to a runner is pulling a hamstring muscle or straining an Achilles tendon. The latter happened to me in high school and was season-ending—I missed my sophomore year of track and field. Paul uses the analogy of a boxer or a runner training for the Olympics (1 Corinthians 9:24 ff). If he doesn't discipline himself by keeping the weight under control and staying fit, he may not win the prize. He doesn't compete with uncertainty; that is, he knows the goal. Tying together the analogies from the letters to Philippians and Corinthians, the goal or prize is *"the upward call of God in Christ Jesus."* He forgets the things that are behind and reaches forward, pressing toward the goal. Drawing from my competition as a distance runner (believe it or not, the life lessons from that experience stick with you through the years), the idea conveyed is of a runner straining to reach the finish line, to be the first to break the tape or edge out the nearest competitor. It is not that we are competing for better standing with God. Instead, it is about the kind of discipline we need to keep our flesh in subjection and to finish the race well.

The 1 Corinthians 9 passage does not refer to losing our salvation. In running competition, there are a few ways that you can be disqualified or disapproved by the race official. One is to jump the gun (a false start by going before the race official fires the starter pistol). If you do it two times, you are disqualified from the race. For a distance runner, it is inexcusable to do this because you have considerably more opportunity to make up for lost time than those in a sprint race. Another way to get disqualified is to leave the track or become entangled with another runner. If you caused it, you're out! To include the boxer analogy from verse six, all of us have let down our guard from time to time. And it has cost us. The devil clobbers us when we slip into worldliness that takes us away from a daily walk with Jesus. Or we endure the loss of respect and trust from others when we fail to do our jobs in the most diligent manner. Sometimes it requires bringing our mind, body, and spirit in subjection fully to the task. I have felt the sting of failure from being intemperate.

In high school, when my teammates and I trained for cross-country season, the first three weeks were always the most grueling. Our coach didn't go easy on us. Within a few days, he had us running country roads for eight or nine miles as our workout after the school day. Our feet were not accustomed to that, so blisters were a common ailment that only made the next day's workout more difficult. Because I had a morning paper route (four miles long, done on my bicycle and on foot) and the rigors of a couple backpacking trips with my dad during the summer, I was in some better shape to start the season than many of my teammates, but competitive racing still required bringing my body into subjection. Many think that running long distances is more a matter of physical conditioning, but the physical conditioning and success that come with it is much more a matter of your mind convincing your body to keep on going and pushing yourself just a little more beyond what you think is your limit. It isn't a matter of the power of positive thinking like the pop psychology fad of a couple decades ago. Attitude is good in any endeavor, but it doesn't have the power of a disciplined life behind it. We subject ourselves to God's will for whatever purposes He may have.

As a runner nears the end of a competitive season, the work of conditioning has paid off if he or she has not given up. In the spring, I was a member of the high school track team where distance runners did both the mile and two-mile races at the same meet with perhaps an hour between events. Of course, these distances have long since been replaced by the metric runs. I remember one race at the end of my junior year that was a qualifier for the state track meet in Idaho. My fastest time in the two-mile until then had been 10 minutes, 32 seconds. It seemed a huge barrier to break. But on that day, it was as if my body was unaware of any pain or discomfort even to the finish line. It seemed I still had some left to give, yet I was 25 seconds faster than my previous best time. Even at that, I did not win the race, but came in fourth or fifth. You see, the other competitors were also much improved by their disciplined work. Just trying to stay with them was enough to boost my time, too.

To extend the analogy, at this point in life, I am in the last lap of my race (the bell lap of a mile run). There are others who will and have outpaced me. Still, Paul admonishes us to run in such a way as to win the race (1 Corinthians 9:24). In other words, don't hold back. In bearing witness of Christ and the kingdom, give it your all. In doing so, we most certainly obtain an imperishable crown. The writer of Hebrews also says that we " . . . *run with endurance the race that is set before us,"* (Hebrews 12:1). We live most effectively by practicing the disciplines of a runner:

1. Lay aside the things that slow us down. (Is it bitterness, unforgiveness or hidden sins?)
2. Run with endurance.
3. Don't look over the shoulder—you might stumble; it is a discipline of the faith to forget about past victories, failures, and losses (Philippians 3:13)
4. Run with confidence in Christ.
5. Encourage others in the race to improve their performance for the kingdom.
6. Discipline your body (and mind).

Aim High

When I ponder the things that really matter in life, the recurring thought is that I should be about doing what brings pleasure to God. Eric Liddell, the Scottish Olympic runner and missionary to China in the mid-20th century, famously said, "When I run, I feel God's pleasure." For him, it was the thing that set him on a worldwide stage to proclaim faith in Christ. It is amazing when we discover for ourselves what that particular thing is by which God is most pleased and glorified. I think it can also change as you get older, finish one thing and move on to another. Along the way, don't linger in thought about how many people will remember you when you die (or how many will be at your funeral). Set your sights on finishing all that Jesus had for you to do and then leave with the understanding you will soon be forgotten but He will be glorified in your part of kingdom work done.

This applies to the many callings God has on each of our lives, not leaving out anything: our marriages, our singleness, our profession, our preaching or teaching of the Gospel, our child rearing, our spiritual gifting and a myriad other ways that we go for this imperishable crown of which Paul speaks. And what about the desert as a calling from God? That is, when He says, "Come to the desert for a season," do you answer the call, or do you hesitate? Do you say, "I don't know, Lord . . . I don't really want that interruption in my life."?

Once there, times will come when you desperately want the desert to end because you fear that you might soon become carrion for the young eagles (well, vultures would be more common there, but we will let that go for this analogy). As I neared the end of my engineering career, my bosses asked me to be a mentor for young engineers. I was happy to do that because I wanted to help those who were on their way up and give something back to the profession. Though expecting them to welcome my advice, some called into question my judgment and experience. On one occasion, a young engineer asked me to review a few drawings and comment on quality, correct content, etc. Keep in mind that at this point I have nearly 25 more years of experience than he, often learned from my own errors and omissions. After presenting a few remarks for him to consider, I got immediate push back on some of them instead of graciously accepting the advice for which he asked.

Later, a relatively inexperienced construction superintendent in our company began a campaign of intimidation when I refused to agree with a contractor's request for extra payment on a claim which was at least borderline fraudulent. The young man argued repeatedly and would not consider compromise. I got agreement from his department manager to negotiate a small settlement based on my examination of the facts. I was just about to present these findings when I learned that the young man had persuaded his boss to go behind my back and agree to full payment of the claim without further discussion with me, the project manager (this role has ultimate responsibility for project budgets and a fiduciary duty to protect company funds). My frustration only deepened when I got virtually no support from my boss because of a well-established 'good ol' boy' network among managers. You could argue that it was sour grapes over egregious office politics, but there was a real feeling of being an inconvenience, getting in the way of someone's agenda.

It is especially humiliating to be the pawn in office politics where your age and experience don't mean what they used to, the kind that we read about in the Book of Proverbs. For better or worse, I am not a political person. I prefer to live by this advice:

> *If it is possible, as much as depends on you, live peaceably with all men.* (Romans 12:18)

But Jesus also admonished us,

> . . . *be wise as serpents and harmless as doves.* (Matthew 10:16)

Adding both together means picking our battles wisely and otherwise trying your best to get along with others. Aim high.

Along with all of that, who hasn't fought the temptation to covet someone else's status or accomplishments in life? In me, it is usually envying others who got promotions throughout their career while I continued to stumble . . . even when I did good work and didn't see it rewarded. And then, at the end of my career, I look back and see that I didn't design any great works of civil engineering or even have a small part in a project like that. Most of what I did was engineering feasibility studies to present alternatives for management decision-making on projects that were best for the business. Fully half of those were never funded or built. But that was an important role, even if it was not the most rewarding career path. Civil engineering is such a broad discipline; it is difficult to be recognized unless you specialize in a particular branch (think bridge design or wastewater treatment). So when I saw friends and other professional acquaintances rise into the ranks of management, my pride was wounded. I struggled with those thoughts that made me feel inadequate or that I was somehow missing out. Never mind that most people never make supervisor or manager rank.

All of this makes me think about the virtue in doing one's work well and, even more, excelling in it. I think this partly answers the question of who rises to the top and who doesn't. Many people stall out somewhere along the way. Proverbs 22:29—the key is excelling in what you do—becoming very good at your craft, trade, or profession. Pay attention to detail. You will be among the well- known and gain great respect from it. Paul was such a man—a Pharisee who knew the law backward and forward, who was fluent in Greek, Hebrew, and Aramaic. Yet having reached that pinnacle of so-called success, he reminds us that knowing (ginosko = understand intimately) Christ far exceeds any other knowledge or success in life.

It never takes long for the Holy Spirit to remind me,

> *. . . we dare not class ourselves or compare ourselves with those who commend themselves. But they, measuring themselves by themselves, and comparing themselves among themselves, are not wise.* (2 Corinthians 10:12)

The point of this verse is that we are not wise when we compare our status with anyone else's. If you can continually practice that truth, you will have peace and contentment. Scripture forces us to look at our own lives and focus on what God wants to change in us. Not only is the desert a time of getting to know God, it is also a time to let God change us, to mold us more in His design. Again, aim high.

Remember Some Things

I touched on this briefly in chapter 2. At times, it helps to remember what God has done on a grand scale throughout human history. It also helps to acknowledge what He has done for you individually. Men, if you are being tempted by a wandering eye in a desert time, try remembering the early days of meeting your wife. Though my love for my wife has grown through the years (if your love is genuine, how can it not?), it does my heart good to remember the early days when our acquaintance was budding into friendship, then blossoming into romantic love. But it started as her idea, pursuing this nerdy boy who did not know up from down in relationships with girls . . . but who knew a good thing when he saw it. I was a Boy Scout and grew up with five brothers, no sisters. That she was interested in me was an astounding realization.

Today, after almost 50 years, I still can look at her and remember that attractive teenager who awakened me to love and excited me so much back then. Of course, we are not the same people now. Our personalities haven't changed much, but our bodies have changed dramatically. We have been molded by life experiences. So my advice to men is to look tenderly at your wife and remember her as the innocent yet exciting girl of your youth while you grow old together, suffering the ravages of time. After all, she went through everything with you.

I also like to remind myself of how my parents prepared me well for days in the desert, though unwittingly for the most part. Our many vacation trips into the wilds taught their boys self-reliance as well as teamwork, looking out for each other, facing fear and overcoming it, struggling against obstacles both mental and physical, even going 'off the trail' to see and experience things you wouldn't have otherwise. By this, I mean going over boulder fields or up steep rockslides on a mountain. This also taught us that those so-called shortcuts to your destination were not always wisely chosen. We learned survival skills and the simplest forms of entertainment like playing hearts (with miniature cards to cut down on weight) and listening to dad's very amateur but amusing harmonica performances around the campfire. It was probably good that my mom wasn't with us on most of those outings, though she was resigned to their good purpose in making men out of boys.

There were other more subtle things inculcated by them. I realized several years after their passing how much I was like them in certain ways. I remembered how they never openly demonstrated anger or spoke harsh words about any of their sons. Oh, my dad's philosophies and world view were different than mine, but we both tried to not let it get in the way of our relationship.

So in those times when I have been tempted to deal harshly with unkind words to family members, I try to be more restrained. My parents' gentle way of molding their offspring has kept me, at times, from inflicting wounds I would most certainly later regret. This isn't to discount the influence of the Holy Spirit in a believer's life, but God used my parents to teach me very important things about how to treat other people. My dad's love definitely was not *phileo*, the affectionate kind. My mom filled that role and brought culture into our lives. My dad's love was more like *agape*, caring for the needs of his sons and demonstrating what was important in life. These lessons have been valuable in desert stretches when I otherwise found relationships with people so discouraging.

Dealing With Bitterness and Forgiveness

The issues of bitterness and forgiveness deserve some attention for the man or woman in the desert because we often struggle with hard feelings toward people who have neglected us or forgotten about us in this time. It is human nature to judge other people for their faults or actions and quite human to struggle with forgiveness. I found my own resentments never directed at my circumstances, but at the people who were instrumental in putting me in them or even those people who showed no compassion for my situation. I confess to letting those thoughts fester at times, which led to the Holy Spirit convicting me about my own motives and bitterness.

Take a look at the New Testament letter to the Hebrews. The author warns us to be careful

> . . . *lest any root of bitterness springing up cause trouble,*
> *and by this many become defiled.* (Hebrews 12:15)

What is this saying? The word picture here is of a root or tuber (Greek *rhiza,* from which we get our word rhizome) such as would be gathered for food, but this one is poisonous. When it sprouts from underground,

131

someone needs to identify it by its features and avoid it. Think what misery it would cause to others in your company who ate it along with you. In a practical sense, this verse is teaching us that hidden resentments can spring up and possibly hurt other people or at least end up driving them away from you.

Along the way, you will find it important also to fight cynicism or you will end up bitter. Worse yet, you will be depressed if pessimism wins.

Have I said this yet—that I am just an amateur theologian (knowing just enough to make me dangerous)? But please allow me now to take a stab at the theology of forgiveness. Of course, entire books have been written about forgiveness. I address it only briefly because most people in the desert must confront the necessity of it in their own journey. And it has been wisely said that unforgiveness (and bitterness) is like drinking poison, all the while expecting the offending person to die from it. I have struggled with the following Gospel passages most of my life as a Christian. I think anyone who doesn't struggle with them has not fully understood them.

In what we call the Lord's Prayer, Matthew and Luke address forgiveness in slightly different ways. In Matthew 6:12, we read *"forgive us our debts . . ."* Translated from *opheillema*, it is figuratively what we would call "garden-variety debt." This might be more simply understood when we include verse 14 in the context of the passage, *"For if you forgive men their trespasses . . . "* and translated from *paraptoma*. Here we are again with the familiar Greek prefix *para*. It is a sideslip, an unintentional error. Picture someone on a slick path that has trouble keeping his footing. This is a refreshing perspective since we all commit this kind of wrong daily in a misspoken word or hurting someone's feelings without knowing it. They might be viewed as sins of omission––we didn't do something good when we had opportunity. Jesus says when we get to the place where we don't take offense for things that people do because we fall down many times, we truly come to understand what God's forgiveness means. It is not that God only forgives us when we forgive others. That doesn't even comport with what we know of God. Rather, it is in forgiving the debts of others that we realize how much we have been forgiven by God.

Luke's account of the model prayer says,

> *And forgive us our sins* (hamartia)*, for we also forgive everyone who is indebted* (opheilo) *to us.* (Luke 11:4)

The latter has the accounting sense of these garden-variety debts accruing or piling up with the suggestion that we know a little about how forgiveness works. *Hamartia* is missing the mark so as not to get the prize. First, I don't think we are dealing with the 'big' sins in these passages. Bearing false witness, murder, adultery, coveting . . . these are usually premeditated acts against others and in violation of God's law. We can all agree that these are not garden-variety sins. But even without those, we have many unintentional slip-ups daily. And even when we aim for the bullseye of moral perfection, we miss because of our sin nature. Sometimes we miss by a lot and other times, just a little. It is to show us that we can't do it. We need God to reconcile the account, and He did this with the sacrificial offering of Jesus, the Son of God.

When people sin against us, as sinful people ourselves we find it difficult to forgive, don't we? When others offend just our sensibilities, we try to hold back forgiving them. It might be evidenced by giving them the silent treatment or even withholding love. In these later years of my life when my flesh wants to lash out at an act that I consider disrespectful perhaps from someone as close as my own children, I try to resist that temptation and remind myself that being mad at them is really a waste of time. They need my help and love first. Remember, that we are made in the image of God and part of that is His immutable attributes of mercy and forgiveness.

Let's consider another passage. Most of Matthew chapter 18 is about forgiving. Matthew had just finished with Jesus' teaching about how to handle the matter of a brother who sins against you. Luke deals with the same subject in abbreviated fashion, but the same point is made. That is, when a brother or sister who has sinned against you asks for forgiveness, you are obligated to forgive if he or she is repentant. It requires some sincerity on their part, but it also means you must respond with sincere forgiveness. Matthew implies the need for sincerity on the part of the offender by going through the contingencies of dealing with a hardened heart (Matthew. 18:15-17).

Next, Peter asks Jesus how many times it was necessary to forgive someone who sins (*hamartano*) against us. Peter thinks seven might be enough. Some have taught that he used seven because it is the number corresponding to perfection in Hebrew thought. Perhaps he reasoned there must be some practical limit to tolerance of errant human behavior. Jesus blows that away with some simple arithmetic. Seventy times seven! "Really?" we would ask. And even if we don't say it, we are thinking this is just hyperbole. Then beginning in 18:23, he uses a parable to contrast our limit to God's limit. The king in this story forgives his servant's 10,000 talent debt while the servant is unwilling to forgive even a 100 denarii debt owed him by a coworker. A single talent was the equivalent of perhaps 6,000 denarii (one denarius being a day's wage for the working-class man or woman). You can do the math from there. Hyperbole again? Not in God's economy of forgiveness.

I think we reconcile these passages of Scripture in this manner. The current majority view of biblical scholarship on forgiveness appears to be forgiving any offenses without any acknowledgment or repentance on the part of the offender. But this is not how our God forgives, is it? Does He just forgive sin whenever and wherever it is committed against Him without the sinner's confession? I don't think that is a right understanding of Scripture. For our part, those little offenses that people do should be forgiven and forgotten. We have no choice but to do that lest we get trapped in an endless cycle of bitterness. But those things done intentionally to harm are a different matter. That requires repentance and seeking forgiveness. At that point, forgiveness should be granted, even if it is a process. Are there gray areas? Yes. There are also areas where sin is committed against God alone, so forgiveness needs to come from Him alone. For example, a man might be guilty of lusting after a woman, but if that's as far as it goes, he doesn't seek her forgiveness. It is a sin before God alone.

It also isn't right to grant forgiveness with conditions attached when someone genuinely seeks it. If you say, "I will forgive, but never speak to that person again," it isn't genuine forgiveness. That isn't to say you don't set boundaries, if needed. Sometimes that is necessary when people are working out differences of opinion or personality clashes.

But what do you do when cornered by the need to forgive someone and you don't really want to do it? Lack of forgiveness is the seed of bitterness. Bitterness is truly a killer of the heart (think literally, heart disease). Pride (hurt feelings) is a strangler of relationships. Envy builds a wall of irrational hatred. For some helpful insights on forgiveness, I recommend reading a 2017 devotional article by Andre Seu Peterson from World News Group. In it, she says,

> "Forgiveness is a brutal mathematical transaction done with fully engaged faculties. It is my pain instead of yours. I eat the debt. I absorb the misery I wanted to dish out on you and you go scot-free." (The World and Everything in It, wng.org, Podcast - October 23, 2017, quote transcribed April, 2018)

I have heard it said that we ought to live without regret. I don't think that is possible. One of my regrets is having said or done something to offend a friend or family member. We have all done this at one time or another whether unwittingly or with intended malice. Even when we forgive those offenses done to us, it doesn't change the offending person. It changes you. Until that offending person is ready to reconcile, you may be wasting time trying to do so. Pray earnestly that God would so change both your heart and theirs that you will be able to come together with love and appreciation for one another again. Don't try to 'fix' things on your own. It is painful to be separated and not speak for years to those you once loved especially if you are from the same tribe. But to ignore prayer in the matter first will leave you or the other party not seeing the elephant in the room when you try to patch things up on your own. This isn't to say that God doesn't expect us to do anything, but timing is important.

The Discipline of Prayer

Remember that the battle we are waging is spiritual in nature, so don't surrender. Paul said we aren't fighting against flesh and blood. We stop struggling through prayer as the praying gets tough because we don't see it answered the way we want or in the time we expected. You know, "God, you sure are taking your time here!"

Far from lying dormant, the spirit of God is taking what we say in prayer and groaning to the Father in words we just cannot get out. This is the essence of Romans 8:26. Maybe all you can say is, "God, I hurt." It is the intercessory work of the Spirit on our behalf. The original word is stenagomois. See the first part, stenag? As noted in chapter 3, this alludes to the work of a secretary taking dictation. You might think of it in our idiomatic way as 'reading between the lines.' The Holy Spirit is never at a loss for words on our behalf.

When you don't feel like praying, it is at least partly because you feel powerless. For example, you may be one of those who is experiencing a sort of self-imposed shame at the feeling that your own children are not making the effort to include you in their lives; worse yet, that they have jettisoned the Christian faith they once embraced as a child under your wing. Your shame makes you want to hide in the wilderness though you don't understand what you did wrong. You want to act, to somehow correct things, but you find your words rebuffed. Now, you realize, you must go to a higher position of power and that position is on your knees.

The Discipline of Reading

People these days have quick access to almost any kind of entertainment from dozens of news channels to movies past and present to easily accessible music or the talking heads on the internet, television and the radio. Without doubt, we live in a distracted age. What we lose in the pursuit of all this, is quiet contemplation and intellectual stimulation that comes from reading good books. Certainly, I include many of the classics as good books, but especially for the Christian, I recommend picking up a book on theology occasionally. The best ones are written for the person in the pew, that also contain some practical application to his or her life. In my desert travel, I read and reread one on the Trinity. At Christmastime, I usually read an astronomy article about the star that guided the Magi to Bethlehem.

Paul wrote an easily overlooked instruction to Timothy:

> *Till I come, give attention to reading.* . . (1 Timothy 4:13)

At the least, he was talking about reading the Old Testament scriptures. Volumes of books were not readily available then. But I don't think it wrong to extrapolate from that the importance of setting aside time to read for the sake of staying informed and to cultivate the mind of Christ in us. Even three or four pages at bedtime will add up.

The Discipline of Praise

What do you think of praise as a discipline? What about learning to praise Him *"yet more and more"* in your desert times (Psalm 71:14)? Now, I was not brought up in any religious tradition that practiced praise in worship or prayer. It was all very reserved . . . and certainly no raising of the hands! Later in life, I began to understand praise and worship more in line with Scripture. There are all kinds of traditions to suit everyone's taste, so I will not say mine is better than someone else's. I am still somewhat reserved in my public expression of praise and worship. Look at Psalm 145 and learn some secrets from King David, the author. He certainly can be trusted to know a few things about it, including praise in the desert of life. In this psalm, I found that praising

God is a many-splendored thing. The English language has few words that derive from the Hebrew, so when you read this psalm, it is good to dig into the many different expressions of praise therein:

Vs. 1a - <u>extol</u>, from *ruhm* (pronounced somewhat like "room"). We sometimes speak of extoling the virtues of something. It means 'to raise up.' Have you ever thought about lifting up God's name? When we elevate Yahweh in our thoughts and words, we are affirming that He is higher than anything, both in our individual lives and in all of creation.

Vs. 1b - <u>bless</u>, from *barak*. This is literally, to kneel as an act of adoration. As such, it is a physical act. It is a humble position, one that acknowledges our sin and our need for mercy while giving due honor to our King. The actual physical motion of kneeling does much to bring our hearts into a humble position before God. We should practice this more often. David says he will do it every day!

Vs. 2 - <u>praise</u>, from *halal*. This is our familiar expression from which we get hallelujah, "praise to God." David says he will do it forever and ever. In a practical sense, this means without giving thought to time.

Vs. 4a - <u>praise</u>, from *shabach* and vs. 4b - <u>declare</u>, from *nagad*. The former is literally to address in a loud tone; the latter is to boldly speak. One generation speaking to the next boldly and loudly, confidently and <u>not</u> quietly. Isn't this our duty? If we accomplish nothing else in life, shouldn't we make it our duty to proclaim and teach the truth about God to the next generation? Notice that even this is an act of worship. Specifically, the psalmist wants us to emphasize God's mighty acts and works. We should engage our minds and memories regularly here. Dig into our knowledge of God's past acts on behalf of His people and on our behalf. What mighty acts has He done for you? Did He save your marriage? Did someone you have been praying for finally accept Christ as Savior? Those are mighty acts! And when I think of His works, it is easy to recall creation. Just take a walk and marvel at the intricacies of everything around you. Then you will give up any doubts you had about a designer of the universe instead of evolution.

Vs. 5 - <u>meditate</u>, from *siyach*. This is to talk to oneself or ponder. We go from the loud expression of God's mighty works to just a personal pondering of them. In fact, one cannot adequately express God's majesty to others without first thinking deeply about it. Reading Scripture aloud to oneself is a form of meditation. Memorizing portions of the Bible is another way to meditate on the Word of God.

Vs. 6b - <u>declare</u>, from *caphar* (saw-far'). This means, to recount intensely or enumerate. Express His greatness in as many ways as you can. Don't just sing the same chorus over and over. Put your mind to the task of remembering how great He is. One simple way to do this that I have found helpful is to remember some of the things God has done for you. The birth of my children is still a lasting memory for me. It was amazing seeing for the first time what God had knit together in the womb—so tiny and vulnerable, but beautiful. We need to recall things like this to keep us going through the desert journeys of our lives.

Vs. 7a - <u>utter</u>, from *naba* (naw-bah'). This is 'to gush forth.' What a great way to describe another aspect of praise! David must be picturing some canyon dry wash in his own desert wanderings that came alive following a storm. This time, it's about remembering His goodness, but you could gush forth about His mercy or His lovingkindness or his Word. When the Spirit of God stirs you, gush forth!

Sometimes the lesson is most easily taught by observing an American robin. God designed this bird to be an expert worm finder. You see it hopping around a grassy yard, occasionally cocking its head as if to listen carefully. Then, it quickly thrusts its beak into the ground and skillfully extracts a worm. Once satisfied with this morsel, it flies to the nearest twig or housetop and starts praising God with its warble––just doing what God designed them to do for the occasion (see also Matthew 6:26).

Vs. 7b - <u>sing</u>, from *ranan* (raw-nan'). This is a shout or sound of joy. It is exercising our vocal cords in a song of praise. We should give it our best voice and perhaps train our voices by practice. Most of us are accustomed to doing this in the congregation of God's people more than when we are off by ourselves. But I don't think there is any excuse for not doing it just because we "can't carry a tune in a bucket."

Vs. 10 - praise, from *yadah*. Again our English translations don't do this proper credit. This word means 'to use the hand.' Here is where most of us struggle because we are afraid of looking too charismatic. If you aren't doing it for show, there is no reason to be self-conscious or ashamed. It is an expression of our surrender to God. Just as David danced before the Lord at the return of the Ark of the Covenant, God wants us to give praise to Him not only with our tongues, but with our bodies—always reverentially, of course. You can raise your hands high or hold them low. God knows the heart.

Vs.21 - speak, from *dabar* (daw-bar') and praise from *tehillah*. The combination of these two is the arrangement of words in a hymn of laudation (an old word we don't use much anymore). In this verse, we see the importance of singing hymns. I think our generation has overemphasized the singing of contemporary choruses in public worship while overlooking hymns written long ago. I am curious to find out what our early church brothers and sisters sang in their congregations. We have no record of it. The words in a song are important. While it's OK to have some contemporary favorites that lift our spirit, I think it is helpful in the desert to have a repertoire of hymns that are theologically rich. Then you are rehearsing truth in the form of praise to the Lord!

Finally, Wright says this of praise in the context of worship:

> "The experience of worship provides the deep resources we need to draw on when everything around falls apart. In worship the emphasis and focus are not on the person but on God. Do you realize that your theology will affect how you respond to loss? Your response to life's losses will be directly determined by your understanding of God and how you have worshiped. We are people who usually put faith in formulas. We feel comfortable with predictability, regularity and assurance. We

want God to be this way too, so we try to create Him in the image of what we want Him to be and what we want Him to do." (*Recovering from Losses in Life*, H. Norman Wright, copyright 1991, republished 2006, Fleming H. Revell Co., p 158)

What's a Dollar Worth in the Desert?

When your desert experience in life includes what some would call periods of financial insecurity, your temptation is to spend more time thinking and, more than likely, worrying about money. Jesus said,

> *In the world* (kosmos) *you will have tribulation* (thlipsis = pressure, John 16:33)

Certainly, financial pressure is part of that. In a familiar passage, Jesus talks about

> *where your treasure is, there your heart will be also.* (Luke 12:34)

In this life, some gain fortunes, some lose them, and most just live in varying degrees somewhere in between. It is striking to me that this matter of money in our lives is an age-old issue. Up to this point in my life, of course, I had become firmly entrenched in the workaday world of making money and planning for the future when I would not be in the workforce in the conventional sense. For me, that meant in some way storing up treasure, all the while knowing that none of us can predict the future with certainty. Still, it's what we have become accustomed to in America. Some squander what they have been given as was the case with the prodigal son in the parable (Luke 15:11-32). Until later in my own dad's life, it didn't make sense that a father would distribute his estate before his death, especially at the beckoning of one son. Interestingly, in those first-century days where a man had two sons, two thirds of his inheritance went to the oldest.

Luke deals with the matter of money several times in his Gospel. Among those passages that I have long pondered for deeper understanding is Jesus' parable about the unjust steward (Luke 16:1-10). In a broad sense here, Jesus is talking about stewardship of truth by using money to illustrate. Jesus is not using the rich man as a metaphor for God the Father. Remember, the rabbinical way of teaching was to compare and contrast from the lesser to the greater, i.e., man is like this, but God is not. He is also making a point about the culture and how it affects our thinking about money. But taken in context with the two parables in Luke chapter 15 where we learn of God's extravagant love for people, in Chapter 16, Jesus is challenging us about what we do with that truth. Do we squander it?

When we read the story itself, we are puzzled by the actions of the unjust steward when, after being fired, he goes about conniving a way to secure his financial future by further defrauding his master in renegotiating debt contracts. Reading between the lines, this occurs without the master's knowledge. It benefits the steward because, in Jewish culture of that time, the axiom was, 'You scratch my back, I'll scratch yours.' If someone did you a favor, you returned it in some way. So now the debtors were further indebted to the steward. You might say, "Why didn't the master just void those agreements?" Probably because that would have made for bad publicity. In any event, we are further perplexed when he commended the steward (just thinking to himself) for such a shrewd business move, even though it cost him a fortune. Now the steward had multiple options for his future and none of them included manual labor.

John MacArthur makes the point about this parable by contrast. Those of the world look at securing their future by gaining wealth and storing up earthly treasure at any cost . . . just to enjoy a few years at the end in tranquil retirement or some such thing. It's what they think about most of the time and the end justifies the means. Shrewd business deals that might take advantage of others unethically or maybe even illegally are all on the table (Grace to You website, gty.org, sermons, Luke 16:1-13, January 15, 2006, accessed January 11, 2020). To that, I add, you might be the one targeted for a layoff rather than the 'good ol' boys' in the business that have more political influence.

On the other hand, those of the kingdom of God should look at using money to secure the future reception of others into heaven. Jesus implies in verse 9 that investing money in the work of bringing others to the kingdom brings the greater reward of seeing them as a reception committee there when you arrive. Your presence there is also probably the result of someone else's investment of money or effort in reaching out to you. This has obvious practical implications even to the individual without great financial resources. Just think of the many ministries with global reach whose mission is to bring aid to desperate situations and then follow with the message of the Gospel. I think most of us can put aside even a little for that kind of thing as God leads. He even says, if we start with that (faithful in little), we will also become faithful in bigger things for the kingdom.

Don't ever entertain the mistaken notion that kingdom work is not costly. It will always cost us something. That is the way God intends it. It is valuable, and He expects a return from us. Why else would Jesus say,

> *To everyone who has, more will be given, and he will have abundance; but from him who does not have, even what he has will be taken away.* (Matthew 25:29)

From Matthew chapter 6, we read Jesus' words about having an evil eye or a good eye (Gr, *opthalmos* from which we get our word opthalmologist—an eye surgeon). This is another of those biblical idioms best explained for our cultural understanding this way—the word has a figurative meaning of envy; that is, looking at someone who has more money makes you want it for yourself. The context of this and surrounding verses is investing for the kingdom. Do we view money as something to envy, or do we want it to do good as an investment in God's kingdom work? Perhaps more broadly, how do we view life? Are we stingy in giving of ourselves and our earthly treasures? Here, perhaps, is a practical application. Do you have a burden to financially support a particular ministry that has the purpose of pushing back against the world's attempts to silence Christian thought and morality, perhaps a legal ministry or an apologetics ministry? Then give generously to that work if you have the means.

Fortunately, the Bible has much to say about the subject of money. By delving into the Proverbs, I found many tidbits that I interpreted for personal application. Though my thoughts are probably not original, they might be valuable in offering perspective on this fundamental aspect of living, especially when it is part of your desert circumstances. You might say it is part of a desert survival tool kit. You will find this in Appendix II.

Help From the Preacher

For the person in the desert, there is no better resource than the Old Testament book of Ecclesiastes. It contains some cynicism, some pessimism, and some reality check. It is viewed by some as the rantings of one who has been jaded by life's many trials and travails. The title of the book comes from the Greek translation of the Old Testament (Septuagint - "translation of the seventy") and means an assembly of people. The author calls himself 'the preacher' but he is King Solomon, passing along more street-level wisdom beyond the book of Proverbs. I am soothed by its contents because I believe Solomon himself experienced the desert of life as much as, or more than, any man. He is perhaps like today's billionaire hedge fund manager or Silicon Valley entrepreneur who has it all—fame, fortune, success and all that comes with them. But there is still an emptiness that he realizes only God can fill.

Here are some things I distilled from a study of Ecclesiastes that I hope will bring a balanced perspective to the reader in desert times, but I advise you to mine the verses on your own for undiscovered treasure:

1. Vs. 1:15, 3:11, and 8:17 – We can't even come close to understanding or knowing everything there is to know. After a long prophecy about Israel in the last days Daniel wrote in the sixth century BC,

Seal the book until the time of the end; many shall run to and fro and knowledge shall increase. (Daniel 12:4)

In case you didn't realize it, that is a verse for our times. The word 'run' implies traveling over the seas. The explosion of knowledge, scientific discovery, and inventiveness is unparalleled in human history. Still, there is no man that can comprehend all of it.

2. Things in life that give only fleeting satisfaction:

- Laughter (2:2) – to be witty and find only the funny things in life to occupy us. It's not wrong to get a laugh from life or a favorite comedy act. From time to time we must laugh at ourselves. After all, Solomon himself said that laughter is like medicine. But it isn't going to work for all our troubles. Matthew Henry's comment on the word 'madness' is that a preoccupation with laughter can lead to estrangement from God. (Matthew Henry's Commentary on the Whole Bible, Hendrickson Publishers Inc., Copyright 1991, 10th printing 1999, pg. 1031)

- Mirth (2:1, 2) – Matthew Henry defines this as preoccupation with sports or recreation as diversion from the toil of life (ibid above). Think of the aristocrats daily hunting their fox like you would see in the movies. It might even be fishing all the time. Nothing wrong with that if you have the time, but eventually you are going to get tired of it.

- Alcoholic drink (2:3) – even if we think we are controlling ourselves in its consumption.

- <u>Materialism</u> (2:4-11, 5:10) – Solomon enumerates the gardens and trees and herds and birds and servants that he acquired; all symbols of wealth in his time. In fact, he is clear in stating,

  Whatever my eyes desired, I did not keep from them.
  (Ecclesiastes. 2:10)

We must be careful about stuff consuming our lives.

3. Ch 3:1-8, 14 – Both good times and hard times in life are designed by God to fulfill a purpose—mainly to draw men to worship Him.

4. Ch. 3:14 – God has put the longing for eternal life in all of us.

5. Ch. 4:8 – The more we work for things, the more we want, even if we have nobody that will inherit them when we die.

6. Ch. 4:9-12 – We need the help of others to get through life's troubles.

7. Ch. 5:1-7 – Watch what you say before men <u>and</u> God. Talking a lot just to be heard and looking busy all the time leads to strange dreams (Your mind trying to reconcile all this activity while you sleep).

8. Ch. 5:8-9 – Don't trust governments of men to right every wrong. Rulers are mere men with the same basic needs as others.

9. Ch. 6 – The search for satisfaction in the material things of this life only starves the soul because there are so many circumstances that bring futility to our efforts.

10. Ch. 7:2-4 – Sorrow is better than laughter. Why would he say this? Is he saying being a pessimist is better than being an optimist? More likely it is that we are made stronger in the painful times of life than the times when things come easy. We also perhaps give things a reality

check. For the desert dweller, this is important because things are not always as they seem, sometimes not even as dire as they appear at first glance.

11. Ch. 7:10 – Don't 'pine for the good ol' days.'

12. Ch. 7:14 – Enjoy the times of prosperity. You know there will be times of adversity. Just remember that God appoints these times for everyone so that we cannot predict the future.

13. Ch. 7:20 – There is no one who is sinless.

14. Ch. 7:21 – Do not worry about every bad thing people say about you. Most of us struggle with this throughout life. We want to be liked by everyone. That is never going to happen. Those who have developed a thick skin for criticism will forge ahead better than those who are easily offended by what others say or think of them. It is the way of the world to put down people with verbal assaults on their character. Maybe it comes from getting older, but I am trying to learn when people say things that are meant to lower me in other's esteem, to think two or three times before opening my mouth in defense. Of course, libel would be an entirely different matter because it has legal implications.

But the people to whom I am referring are usually somewhere in your circle of family or friends. They might even be innocently trying to stir a conversation or add a bit of humor as they see it. So when something unflattering is said about me, I try to think, "Why not me?" instead of, "Why me?" Sooner rather than later, we should realize just how deeply flawed we are. If not for the kindness of God, I would have nothing. This is not to forget those He placed in my path who gave me opportunities I probably didn't merit given my aptitude. I like to joke about my college academic record by saying that I graduated summa cum dummy. After so many years, I realize that I am nothing to brag about. None of us are.

15. Ch. 7:29 – God made man upright, but he is always seeking out sinful schemes. We are made in God's image, but our sinful bent is to think wrong things and sometimes carry them out.

16. Ch.8:5b-6 – As the saying goes, 'timing is everything.' This is especially true in business. But bad things happen, so be aware of how things are changing and how to plan for them. Even Matthew Henry saw it this way in the 17th century saying, "Men are miserable because they are not sufficiently sagacious and attentive." (Matthew Henry's Commentary on the Whole Bible, Hendrickson Publishers Inc., Copyright 1991, 10th printing 1999, pg. 1046)

17. Ch. 9:11 – Time and chance happen to all men (no matter how strong or smart you are).

18. Ch. 9:12 – Evil times come to men without warning.

19. Ch. 10:4 – If those who have authority over you begin to turn against you, don't run. Try to do whatever you can to reconcile whatever caused the problem. This verse caught my attention when I realized it wasn't just applicable in a military context (as it appears in the text). We tend to run from trouble or try to cover up our mistakes. Sometimes it is just better to 'fess up' and try to be conciliatory with a boss or manager. Maybe she doesn't understand why you did it the way you did. Remaining silent can sometimes hurt you because you aren't giving the authorities the help they need to solve the problem. It is easy to become frozen by our errors, thinking there is no way out. You may have to suffer some indignity from a verbal chastisement but being humble and speaking well in a crisis is usually the better path. I had to learn this the hard way . . . long before I caught the application of this verse.

20. Ch. 10:8-10 – Wisely prepare for whatever task you are doing. "He who digs a pit . . . He who quarries stones . . . he who splits wood . . . " are all occupations for some purpose or gain that Solomon is using to

illustrate the importance of planning ahead and carefully executing a task. I know about the last one, having split many cords of wood over the years with a wedge and sledgehammer. It takes some skill, but there is still some risk of injury as there is in almost any human occupation.

21. Ch. 10:15 – This is a curious verse. "The labor of fools wearies them, for they do not even know how to go to the city!" Some people are so lazy they can't even follow a map or directions to get where they need to go!

22. Ch. 10:18 – "Because of laziness, the building decays, and through idleness of hands, the house leaks." Everything needs maintenance. It is the second law of thermodynamics (entropy) at work in our sin-cursed world. Men are creative in their inventions, no doubt about it. Curse it if you want, but everything we build requires some maintenance to keep working the way it was designed. If you hold that perspective, you will be more patient when things break and need fixing.

23. Ch. 10:19b – "Money answers everything." It was just as true in Solomon's day as it is ours—follow the money, and you will get to the root of much of the corruption we see in our world.

24. Ch. 11:1 – "Cast your bread upon the waters, for you will find it after many days." This enigmatic verse is not well-explained from the English translation. After so many years of being stumped, I heard this analogy: think of a ship in a commercial venture of transporting wheat. There are risks like shipwreck, spoilage, theft, and not getting your agreed purchase price. Here I think the adage 'nothing ventured, nothing gained' applies. This is true of all business ventures, though it may take time to become profitable.

25. Ch. 11:2-6 – These verses are connected in context with verse 1 in saying that the events of life are sometimes uncontrollable and irreversible. So don't just stand around doing nothing because you are

afraid of failure. Take some risk in life and help others along the way (vs. 2) because you can't predict the future. I have adopted a corollary to this as one of my hard and fast rules of life—it is rare that something is done right the first time. Work always requires a diligent second effort.

I had a supervisor for a short time who was a chemical engineer. In training me about the process of making silicon, he inadvertently taught me something I have not since forgotten. Theoretically, a chemical reaction will result in quantities of product predicted by stoichiometry. In the actual process, he pointed out that some reactants remained unconverted. He explained it by saying, "It's not a perfect world." Isn't that true in so many of life's endeavors where things don't work out as planned?

26. Ch. 11:8 – Even if life has been good, there will be many days of bad things coming. Count on it!

27. Ch. 12:13-14 – The conclusion of these thoughts on life: fear God and keep His commandments because He is bringing everything into judgement, even things we think are secret.

God's intention in the desert of life is to focus your attention on Him, His Word, and Jesus, the Living Word—to live in constant communion with Him whether days are evil or good.

Losing and Finding our Identity

The final help for the desert that I want to address is our identity. I touched on this earlier in talking about loss. Our identity is tied up in so many things that we can't keep track of them all. Consider just our relationships. If you have moved many times, you know what I am talking about because you never actually stay anywhere long enough to establish lasting, meaningful friendships. It is the way of the desert that you are pushed to the fringe of family and perhaps church relationships without any explanation most of the time. It cuts like a knife across your heart because you must work so hard just to not be left out. You find that forming new bonds is hard because people are reluctant to bring you into their circle. Maybe it is just outside their comfort zone. These are the times you feel the loss of identity. These are the times you <u>must</u> remember your identity in Christ because it is the one thing that will never change.

The desert will wipe you out if you are just there to conquer it. When you drift into that kind of thinking, you begin to lose your identity. The single most important thing for a child of God to grasp and hold on to is his or her identity in Christ. We will not be satisfied trying to gain our identity in the love of money or the adulation that comes from friends and family or fame or success. Those all have the common trait of eventually letting us down. When we cling to our identity in Christ, what the world says or thinks about us will no longer make us insecure. We can go ahead, focused instead on the resurrected Christ and His will for our lives. I have known many people who were so caught up in being right, that they could not pause and listen to what others were saying. Let's not be that way with God. Our roadmap is the New Testament letters of Paul and John. They show us who we are in Christ, so let's take a look.

We are conformed to the image of the Son of God (Rom 8:29). *Summorphos* is used here. We say a caterpillar changes to a butterfly through the biological process of metamorphosis. For the Christian, it is by the new birth that we become a new creation. It isn't just a jargoned phrase that we use. The beauty of it is that we are literally added and reshaped into the likeness (*eikon*) of Christ. We are familiar with icons on computer displays—a symbol that identifies a program (basically the gateway to the program). You could make the point that we, as likenesses of Christ are windows through which others see Christ. In centuries past, the Catholic and Orthodox churches of Europe made much of their ikons—statues, ornaments, paintings, etc. as proof of their identification with Christ.

We are joint heirs with Christ (Romans 8:17). What does an heir get? All that the father bequeaths in his will. We share in our heavenly Father's inheritance because we have been adopted. In fact, Galatians 4:5-7 says we were adopted out of slavery (to sin)—from slaves to heirs in an instant! We get all that comes with the kingdom of God. This has become part of our new identity. But we don't gain this status without legal consent. We get that through the new covenant God made and signed with the blood of Christ.

We are sanctified in Christ and have come into His fellowship (1 Corinthians 1:2, 9). We don't use the term 'sanctify' in modern speech very much. It is a buzzword of sorts among church people in-the-know. It is still an important word, though. It means to be made holy. Most people in our times have even lost understanding of what holiness means. We acknowledge that it is both an instantaneous occurrence and a process throughout our lives. But we don't make ourselves holy. God does that through the work of the Holy Spirit in our hearts. It is instant in the sense that we are cleaned at the new birth and set apart for God. At this point, we also come into fellowship with Christ Himself . . . even before we become part of a church congregation!

We are the temple of God where the Spirt of God dwells (1 Corinthians 3:16; 6:19). We can be guilty of taking this truth for granted. Does He dwell in inanimate objects and animals as eastern mysticism teaches? No, God the Holy Spirit dwells in the person who has surrendered their heart to God the Son. It would help if we woke up every morning and reminded ourselves that the eternal God has made these decaying bodies His dwelling place . . . not just when we are doing well or when we are at our purest and holiest state, but ALL the time and even in the desert. He doesn't leave us, but His presence is real when we seek fellowship with Him in the most barren times.

We belong to Christ and are joined to Him, body and spirit (1 Corinthians 3:23 and 6:15, 17 and 12:27). There is a beautiful word picture here. The word for 'joined' comes from the Greek *kollao*. We get our words collage and collagen from it. We know a collage is a work of art where many different pieces (paper or other material that is cut up from many sources) are combined and glued to a single substrate. Similarly, collagen is connective tissue in body joints, including animals. When boiled in water, it creates glue. All of this to say that the body of Christ is comprised of many different pieces . . . all of them glued to Christ. Paul is teaching this in the moral context of sexual purity, but the larger point is that our bodies and souls are fixed firmly with Jesus' body and spirit. How can this be? It is a wonderful mystery.

We are a letter from Christ written by the Holy Spirit on our hearts (2 Corinthians 3:3). Verse 2 says we are a letter known and read by all men. Remember that when you think that you are not useful to God. No, all your life, you are being viewed by other people. By that, they are learning about Jesus. We don't know much about letter writing in this age of instant communication. It is a lost art. A letter is an intimate form of communication. When my wife and I were in our courtship days, we lived 2500 miles apart while pursuing our college education. We saw each other rarely in these years. Yes, I called on the telephone, but we also exchanged letters, sometimes including a cassette tape so we could hear one another's voices and express our love. Christ is using us as an intimate expression of His love to a lost world.

We are ambassadors for Christ (2 Corinthians 5:20). What is the role of an ambassador? It is to represent the interests of one's country in another nation. Similarly, we represent the kingdom of Christ. If you are in Christ, part of your identity is ambassador. This is a vital position in any government. In the most critical times, such as when there are tensions between nations, the ambassador must implore his host nation to terms of peace to avoid hostilities. Now, our unbreakable citizenship is in heaven (Philippians 3:20), but just like the earthly ambassador, we live in a foreign land until called home by our King. Every earthly consulate is sovereign ground within its host nation. Even so with us. We are protected while in a foreign land doing the work of demonstrating the greatness of our God and His kingdom while making strong entreaties for others to make peace with God as well. Can you see the high position and value of this part of your identity?

We are new creations in Christ (2 Corinthians 5:17). When the enemy is pummeling you with accusations of inadequacy, remember this. At the new birth, you became a new creation. Literally, this is what happened—God came alongside us and peeled away the old sin and its resulting scars, casting it aside like a rotting carcass. We are not going back there again. Throughout 2 Corinthians, Paul uses other imagery to convey this newness in Christ. In Chapter 2, we are fragrance. In Chapter 3, we are being changed by the Holy Spirit into the image of the Lord. In Chapter 6, we are the temple of God. He is encouraging us down through the ages that we are new creations reflective of God's glory. Rejoice daily in this aspect of your identity!

EPILOGUE

When you find yourself in life's desert, has it caused you to run and hide? Has it left you with a sense of hopelessness? God did not intend the desert for that. The God who has revealed Himself in the pages of the Bible wants you to Himself in these times. He wants you to dive into the scriptures, read and study. Get to know who He is. Your journey will be different than mine, your discoveries along the way different also. You will fight with God at times, struggle with Him in a sense as did Jacob. You will find yourself isolated, and it may not feel comfortable. These are the circumstances where God will reveal Himself in ways you never thought possible.

Especially as we grow old, the temptation in our culture is to make sure we have lived life to the fullest, to complete as much of the 'bucket list' as possible (yes, I have one of those too). Instead, why not accept His invitation to walk with Him in the desert times? The Holy Spirit will give you peace and strength through it while you come to a richer understanding of God. I believe this is what He desires from us more than anything, even our best work for His kingdom. In truth, when we develop that closeness, we become more useful for kingdom purposes. As we near the final years of our lives, it becomes more important to know Him and the power of His resurrection because we are close to that meeting day in Heaven. We are preparing to leave this life. Some people become rich. Some become famous, even by means of gifted or extraordinary talent. But our end is all the same. In death, we take nothing of it with us and are forgotten, some sooner than others.

Pray much . . . talk to Him during these times that seem so treacherous. Develop a discipline in that. If you are still in shock at finding yourself in the desert of life, utter what you can. The Holy Spirit has promised to speak to the Father especially in these times when words just will not form on our lips.

God reminds us from time to time that life is short. Those who live to 90 are still the exception. I have been with relatives in recent years that were on special medication or restrictive diets because of a medical condition. These were people under 60 years of age who didn't smoke or drink! Stress may have been a factor, but I realized (as did some of them) that life is too short to work right up to the end. So that trip you always wanted to take with your wife but thought you had to wait until retirement—why not do it now?

Many, I think, take the desert to be some forbidden place—a place where you do not stay any longer than necessary. You must travel through quickly lest you become stranded in the heat of the day. But I say again that God doesn't want your desert days to be wasted. Our lives are so conditioned to be thinking and planning our next venture that we feel guilty thinking any other way. What if God is, instead, calling you to a time of slowness so you can know Him better? Even that will not happen without surrendering your hurriedness. It might be that He wants to use the desert to prepare you for a task that you could not do otherwise (these "greater works' that Jesus speaks of in John 14). Maybe He wants you close as you take the final steps on this earth. It may be for the long journey ahead in life where you will need to know your God intimately to make it all the way. It may seem at times to be a place of affliction, but remember that it is light and temporary compared to the heavy weight of glory awaiting us in the city God is preparing (see 2 Corinthians 4:17, 18).

APPENDIX I

New Testament References Related to Suffering
(Pertaining to Chapter 3)

Dioko (to pursue, specifically as persecution): Matt. 5:11, 5:44, 10:23, 23:34; Luke 21:12, John 5:16, 15:20; Rom 12:14, Gal. 5:11, Phil. 3:14, 2 Tim. 3:12; many other places.

Dokime (test or experiment for proof; trans. as *trial* in KJV): 2 Cor. 8:2

Dokimion (a testing for trustworthiness; trans. as *trial* in KJV): 1 Peter 1:7, 4:12

Kakopatheo (to undergo hardship, be afflicted, suffer trouble): 2 Tim. 2:3, 2:9, 4:5; James 5:10, 13

Pascho (to experience a painful sensation or impression; trans. as *suffer* in KJV): in the Gospels ref. to Christ's sufferings; Matt. 17:15, Acts 1:3, 9:16, 1 Cor. 12:26, 2 Cor. 1:6; Gal. 3:4; Phil. 1:29; 2 Tim. 1:12; 3:14 &17, 4:15, 16 & 19; 1 Th. 2:14; Heb. 2:18, 5:8, 9:26, 13:12 (speaking of Christ); 1 Peter 2:19, 20, 21 & 23, 3:14, 17 & 18, 4:1, 15, 16 & 19, 5:10; Rev. 2:10

Pathema (something undergone as in a hardship or pain; subj. an emotion or influence; trans. as *suffering or sufferings* in KJV): Rom. 7:5, 8:18; 2 Cor. 1:5-7; Phil. 3:10; Col. 1:24; 2 Tim. 1:8; Heb. 2:9, 10, 10:32; 1 Peter 1:11, 4:13, 5:1,9

Peira (a test with the idea of piercing; trans. as *trial* in KJV): Heb. 11:36

Peirasmos (scrutinizing or putting to proof; by implication, adversity; trans. *temptation(s)* in KJV): Matt. 6:13, 26:41; Mk. 14:38; Lk. 4:13, 8:13, 11:4, 22:28, 40, & 46; Acts 20:19; 1 Cor. 10:13; Gal. 4:14; 1 Tim. 6:9; Heb. 3:8; James 1:2 & 12; 1 Peter 1:6; 2 Peter 2:9; Rev. 3:10

Peirazo (to test or scrutinize; trans. as *tempt or tempted* in KJV): Matt. 4:1; Mk. 1:13; Lk 4:2, 20:23; John 6:6; Acts 5:9, 15:10; 1 Cor. 7:5, 10:9 & 13; 2 Cor. 13:5; Gal. 6:1; 1 Th. 3:5; Heb. 2:18 (twice), 3:9, 4:15, 11:37; James 1:13 (once, first ref.), 1:14

Purosis (ignition, specif. as smelting; trans. *fiery* in KJV): 1 Peter 4:12

Stenochoria, stenochoreo (narrowness of room; trans. as *distress, distressed* or *anguish* in KJV): Rom. 2:9, 8:35; 2 Cor. 4:8, 6:4, 12:10

Sumpascho (To experience pain jointly or of the same kind; trans. as *suffer* in KJV): Rom 8:17, 12:26

Thlibo (crowding; trans. as *suffer tribulation, trouble* in KJV): 2 Cor. 4:8; 1 Th. 3:4; 2 Th. 1:6

Thlipsis (pressure; trans. mostly as *affliction or tribulation* in KJV): Matt. 13:21, 24:9, 21 & 29; Mk. 4:17, 13:19 & 24; John 16:21 & 33; Acts 7:10 & 11, 11:19, 14:22, 20:23; Rom. 2:9, 5:3, 8:35, 12:12; 1 Cor. 7:28; 2 Cor 1:4 & 8, 2:4, 4:17, 6:4, 7:4, 8:2 & 13; Eph. 3:13; Phil. 1:16, 4:14; Col. 1:24; 1 Th. 1:6, 3:3, 4 & 7; 2 Th. 1:4 & 6; Heb. 10:33; James 1:27; Rev. 1:9, 2:9, 2:10, 2:22, 7:14

Zemioo (to injure reflexively or passively; to experience detriment; from zemia for experiencing loss in a violent way): Matt. 8:36, Luke 9:25; 1 Cor. 3:15; 2 Cor 7:9; Phil. 3:8

Reference source is *Strong's Exhaustive Concordance of the Bible*, MacDonald Publishing Company, McLean, Virginia

APPENDIX II

Table of Proverbs About Money (From Ch. 6)

Verse	NKJV	My Interpretation
1:19	*So are the ways of everyone who is greedy for gain; It takes away the life of its owners.*	The wicked are sometimes so greedy that it becomes an all-consuming passion.
13:4	*The soul of a lazy man desires, and has nothing, but the soul of the diligent shall be made rich.*	Riches don't come without diligent effort. Or the old adage, 'Most people miss opportunity because it usually shows up in overalls and looks like hard work.'
13:7	*There is one who makes himself rich, yet has nothing;*	Some make themselves look wealthy by spending beyond their means.
13:7	*And one who makes himself poor, yet has great riches.*	The frugal gain wealth, but never look like it.
13:8	*The ransom of a man's life is his riches.*	Riches (sometimes) bring trouble. Others are after your wealth which sometimes requires payoffs.
13:8	*The poor does not hear rebuke.*	Those with no money are not hassled.

14:4	*Where no oxen are, the trough is clean; but much increase comes by the strength of an ox.*	In business, 'nothing ventured, nothing gained;' you have to spend money (on production capital) to make money.
14:20	*The poor man is hated even by his own neighbor, but the rich has many friends.*	Sometimes people are liked just because they have money.
14:23	*In all labor there is profit, but idle chatter leads only to poverty.*	Just talking about doing work will make you poor.
15:16	*Better is a little with the fear of the LORD, than great treasure with trouble.*	It is better to trust in the Lord than to have a lot of money and all the trouble it brings.
16:8	*Better is a little with righteousness, than vast revenues without justice.*	It is better to have little money and live right than to be wealthy and not use money to help people.
18:11	*The rich man's wealth is his strong city, and like a high wall in his own esteem.*	Wealthy people without God think their money is enough to protect them from anything.
18:23	*The poor man uses entreaties, but the rich answers roughly.*	People with more than enough money tend to say whatever they want with impunity and can become callous toward the needy.
20:17	*Bread gained by deceit is sweet to a man, but afterward his mouth will be filled with gravel.*	Getting money by deceitful means might feel good at first, but is like eating gravel when you try to enjoy it.

20:21	*An inheritance gained hastily at the beginning will not be blessed at the end.*	Getting rich quickly doesn't turn out well in the long run (e.g., most lottery winners)
21:5	*The plans of the diligent lead surely to plenty, but those of everyone who is hasty, surely to poverty.*	'Get rich quick' schemes don't work. You build wealth with diligent effort and planning.
21:6	*Getting treasures by a lying tongue is the fleeting fantasy of those who seek death.*	Some people imagine they can get rich by lying, but they are just courting disaster and ruin.
22:2	*The rich and the poor have this in common, the LORD is the maker of them all.*	The rich and the poor are equal in God's sight.
22:7	*The rich rules over the poor and the borrower is servant to the lender.*	In this world system, the independently wealthy often have power over people of lesser means.
22:26	*Do not be one of those who shakes hands in a pledge, one of those who is surety for debts.*	Think before you go into debt. Get everything in writing.
22:27	*If you have nothing with which to pay, why should he take away your bed from under you?*	If you don't have any means of paying a debt, your possessions might be taken away.
23:4	*Do not overwork to be rich; Because of your own understanding, cease!*	For your own sanity, don't be a workaholic to get rich.

23:5	*Riches certainly make themselves wings; They fly away like an eagle toward heaven.*	Riches can be gone quickly, like a bird flying away.
27:23, 24	*Be diligent to know the state of your flocks, and attend to your herds; for riches are not forever.*	Riches are not guaranteed to last. You must pay attention to the state of your business.
28:11	*The rich man is wise in his own eyes.*	Rich people tend to think highly of their own opinions or that their 'smarts' made them rich.
28:22	*A man with an evil eye hastens after riches, and does not consider that poverty will come upon him.*	Those whose sole ambition is to get rich quickly, don't realize how quickly riches can go away.

Made in the USA
Las Vegas, NV
04 March 2023

68518678R00095